HISPANIC TEXTS

general editor
Professor Catherine Davies
Department of Hispanic and Latin American Studies
Nottingham University

series previously edited by
Professor Peter Beardsell, University of Hull
Emeritus Professor Herbert Ramsden

series advisers
Spanish literature: Professor Jeremy Lawrance
Department of Hispanic and Latin American Studies, University of Nottingham
US adviser: Professor Geoffrey Ribbans, Brown University, USA

Hispanic Texts provide important and attractive material in editions with an introduction, notes and vocabulary, and are suitable both for advanced study in schools, colleges and higher education and for use by the general reader. Continuing the tradition established by the previous *Spanish Texts*, the series combines a high standard of scholarship with practical linguistic assistance for English speakers. It aims to respond to recent changes in the kind of text selected for study, or chosen as background reading to support the acquisition of foreign languages, and places an emphasis on modern texts which not only deserve attention in their own right but contribute to a fuller understanding of the societies in which they were written. While many of these works are regarded as modern classics, others are included for their suitability as useful and enjoyable reading material, and may contain colloquial and journalistic as well as literary Spanish. The series will also give fuller representation to the increasing literary, political and economic importance of Latin America.

Soledades. Galerías. Otros poemas

Manchester University Press

HISPANIC TEXTS

also available

Carmen Conde *Mientras los hombres mueren*
  ed. Jean Andrews

Julio Cortázar *Siete cuentos*
  ed. Peter Beardsell

Spanish contemporary poetry: An anthology
  ed. Diana Cullell

Gertrudis Gómez de Avellaneda *Sab*
  ed. Catherine Davies

Elena Poniatowska *Querido Diego, te abraza Quiela*
  ed. Nathanial Gardner

La vida de Lazarillo de Tormes
  ed. R.O. Jones

Lope de Vega Carpio *El Caballero de Olmedo*
  ed. Anthony John Lappin

Ramón J. Sender *Réquiem por un campesino español*
  ed. Patricia McDermott

Pablo Neruda *Veinte poemas de amor y una canción desesperada*
  ed. Dominic Moran

Gabriel García Márquez *El coronel no tiene quien le escriba*
  ed. Giovanni Pontiero

Federico García Lorca *Bodas de sangre*
  ed. H. Ramsden

Federico García Lorca *La casa de Bernarda Alba*
  ed. H. Ramsden

Federico García Lorca *Romancero gitano*
  ed. H. Ramsden

Lorca's Romancero gitano: eighteen commentaries
  ed. H. Ramsden

Miguel Barnet and Esteban Montejo *Biografía de un Cimarrón*
  ed. William Rowlandson

Miguel Delibes *El camino*
  ed. Jeremy Squires

Octavio Paz *El laberinto de la soledad*
  ed. Anthony Stanton

Federico García Lorca *Yerma*
  ed. Robin Warner

Alfredo Bryce Echenique *Huerto Cerrado*
  ed. David Wood

Antonio Machado

Soledades. Galerías. Otros poemas

edited with an introduction, critical analysis, notes and vocabulary by
Richard A. Cardwell

Manchester University Press

All editorial matter, in English and Spanish © Richard A. Cardwell 2015
All other material © as acknowledged

The right of Richard A. Cardwell to be identified as the editor of this work has been asserted by him in accordance with the Copyright, Designs and Patents Act 1988.

Published by Manchester University Press
Altrincham Street, Manchester M1 7JA
www.manchesteruniversitypress.co.uk

British Library Cataloguing-in-Publication Data
A catalogue record for this book is available from the British Library

Library of Congress Cataloging-in-Publication Data applied for

ISBN 978 0 7190 443 0 *paperback*

First published 2015

The publisher has no responsibility for the persistence or accuracy of URLs for any external or third-party internet websites referred to in this book, and does not guarantee that any content on such websites is, or will remain, accurate or appropriate.

Typeset in Adobe Garamond Pro
by Koinonia, Manchester
Printed in Great Britain
by Bell & Bain Ltd, Glasgow

† For Herbert Ramsden,
who taught me to read Spanish Symbolist poetry

Contents

Preface	*page* ix
Introduction	1
Select bibliography	59
Text and notes: *Soledades. Galerías. Otros poemas*	69
Appendix	171
Temas de debate y discusión	175
Selected vocabulary	177

Preface

A number of editions of *Soledades. Galerías. Otros poemas* (*SGOP*) have appeared since the first publication of the collection in 1907. The most reliable date from the late 1960s onwards and especially the editions of Geoffrey Ribbans, Oreste Macrì and José Carlos Mainer. An edition of *Soledades*, the first 1903 version of the collection, by Dolores Romero López offers further detailed information on the genesis of *SGOP*: see the bibliography for details. This edition does not seek to replicate these editions which are rich in research material and trace the genesis of *SGOP* from its earliest poems and the new ones. Rather the aim here is to offer a fuller introduction to the collection freed from the detailed research apparatus these studies offer. This edition specifically sets Machado in the context of his family, his intellectual formation and the literary circles in which he wrote. The primary aim is to present *SGOP* in a simpler form, focusing on a close engagement with the poems themselves and, especially, the intellectual and artistic moment in which they were composed. The edition is directed at teachers and students alike. For those who may be familiar with the text, the Introduction offers a new approach to the poems. There, for both those who have read Machado and those coming fresh to the poet, I explore the poet's early education, his experiences of *fin de siglo* Paris and Madrid, the circles in which he mixed, the personal contacts he made and the aesthetic debates and intellectual currents of the time, all of which came together in the composition of one of the preeminent verse collections of the time. In addition I set the intellectual patterns Machado absorbed in their historical context and trace their origins. Through the Notes to each poem, I explain images, themes and underlying preoccupations, even obsessions. I also include, where relevant, reference to the first publication of the poem and the measure of verse which Machado employs, the majority of them based on popular and traditional forms. References to articles and books dealing with specific aspects discussed in the Introduction and Notes are offered for further study, critical works which may be followed up or simply passed over. These references will be identified by author and date in the text itself, including page numbers where relevant (e.g. Gullón 1960, 54), with full details listed in the bibliography. An extensive vocabulary covering quotations in the Introduction and the poems themselves is provided to aid reading. Translations of single difficult words are included in square brackets in the Introduction itself. Many studies have examined *SGOP* with hindsight, forming judgements from Machado's writings published at a later date. Here the reader is offered the poems in their proper context and in the intellectual moment in which they were created between 1899 and 1907. Thus very little reference to Machado's work after 1907 will be made.

The number of critical works on Machado is considerable though many early studies are unreliable. Various anniversaries, the centenary of Machado's birth in 1975 and half-centenary of his death in 1989, the centenary of *Soledades* in 2003, with special issues of *Ínsula*, núm. 683, and *Humanitas, Revista de la Facultad de Humanidades y Ciencias de la Educación de la Universidad de Jaén*, núm. 3, followed by the centenary of *SGOP* in 2007, for example, have produced a myriad of essays of varying quality. In the bibliography I list those essays and studies which might prove complementary to the present essay or remain classic in Machado criticism. The centenary of Machado's birth was marked by a *Bibliografía Machadiana*, Servicio de Publicaciones del Ministerio de Educación y Ciencia (Madrid: Artes Gráficas Clavileño, 1976). The standard yearly bibliographies in the *Publications of the Modern Language Association of America (PMLA)*, the *Year's Work in Modern Language Studies* and the 'Review of Reviews' in the *Bulletin of Hispanic Studies* and its offshoot, *Bulletin of Spanish Studies*, as well as those in *Nueva Revista de Filología Española*, all offer complementary listings of Machado criticism and new material . The editions of Ribbans (1975 and 1998), Macrì (1988) and Mainer (1995) and the edition of *Soledades* by Romero López, cited in the bibliography, all offer extensive lists of relevant works. Two more recent collections of conference papers offer, among many general studies, articles on Machado's family and the early work: *Antonio Machado hoy*, Jorge

Urrutia (ed.). Actas del Congreso Internacional Conmemorativo del Cincuentenario de la muerte de Antonio Machado (Sevilla: Alfar, 1990), 4 vols (hereinafter *Antonio Machado hoy*) and Jordi Domènech (coordinador), *Hoy es siempre todavía*. Curso Internacional sobre Antonio Machado (Córdoba: Ayuntamiento de Córdoba / Sevilla: Renacimiento, 2006) (hereinafter *Hoy es siempre*). A synthesis of the last twenty years of critical debate can be found in E. Álvarez, 'Estética, ideología y voluntad de poder: el espacio de la modernidad en la poesía de Antonio Machado', *Revista Hispánica Moderna*, 51 (2006), 5–26. The listings in Google Scholar are mostly unhelpful. The bibliography of this edition lists those works of immediate interest to the early work of Machado deemed of interest for further reading. For more advanced reading see the notes in the Introduction and the Notes to the Poems which have further listings and are cited in full in the bibliography.

Machado has been viewed as a solitary poet musing on his own personal and poetical problems. This edition argues to the contrary, viewing Machado as a part of a group of idealistic writers challenging the *status quo* in an age of decline. In what follows I hope to demonstrate that an understanding of Machado's preoccupations, expressed in a subtle idiom, are worthy of study not only as a mirror to the obsessions of the age and in their proper context, but also for the laying bare of the mind and imagination of a young poet caught, as with his contemporaries, between a passing age of formal religion and imperial dreams and a new view of the world in which those ideals seemed wanting.

Introduction

Critical problems in the early work

The extensive list of studies on the early poetry of Antonio Machado y Ruiz (1875–1939) reveal many opinions on an apparently multi-faceted poet. However, despite many readings of particular aspects of Machado's early oeuvre there remain four aspects which have not received due attention. The first is that Machado's intellectual formation is sketchily or rarely explored in depth in relation to the study of his first two collections whose titles suggest a solitary and retiring poet. Moreover, detailed analysis of Machado's education and a critical reading of the two early books tend to be studied separately. Yet his education in Seville and Madrid and, between 1899 and 1902, his two visits to Paris, as much as his contact with a new circle of writers after 1902, shape his outlook and opinions and form the necessary evidence for a proper understanding of *Soledades. Galerías. Otros poemas*. Màtyàs Horànyi, as early as 1975, argued that:

> Un estudio de las primeras producciones poéticas de Antonio Machado debería empezarse, por tanto, con una seria revisión e interpretación de los hechos biográficos anteriores buscando las vivencias, impresiones e influencias que pudieron haber orientado la formación del mundo poético del joven Machado. Esta revisión tiene una importancia especial para la comprensión del primer volumen de Machado, porque la crítica se ocupa menos del fondo biográfico de las *Soledades* que del resto de la obra machadiana. (Horànyi 1975, 7)

Further, Machado's early writings are all too often studied in themselves alone, remote from the aesthetics, ethics, politics and personal contacts of his time. Three notable exceptions are García Blanco (1965, 215–91), Albornoz (1968) and Ribbans (1971) who consider the relationship with Unamuno; Gullón (1959 and 1960) for Jiménez. As a result his place in the ferment of new ideas which emerged in the period 1900–1907 when *Soledades* (1903)[1] (hereinafter *S*) and its expanded version, *Soledades. Galerías. Otros poemas* (1907),[2] (hereinafter *SGOP*) were composed, has been underestimated or largely ignored. Machado at this time, mistakenly, is too often seen as a solitary poet.[3] After the death of his wife Leonor in August 1912, Machado, near to suicide, as he revealed in a letter to Juan Ramón Jiménez shortly after (Macrì 1988, 1519; hereinafter *PrC*), seems to have desired a solitary life 'paseando y leyendo' in Baeza where he had taken a teaching post far away from the memories of Soria, a period only broken when he moved to Madrid and Segovia in the 1920s where, again, he entered the artistic world of the capital. These years of withdrawal and the creation of the heteronymic personae of Abel Martín and Juan de Mairena have led to the view that Machado was deeply involved in his own personal and solitary search for answers to the great metaphysical questions (Baker 1985). But his earlier years in Madrid and Paris in the *fin de siglo* reveal a very different Machado, a poet at the forefront of the literary ferment of the time, a poet in contact with fellow writers who were engaged in a similar campaign to 'regenerate' the nation and their fellow men (Romero López 2006, 7; Correa Ramón 2006). This fact is immediately relevant to *S* and *SGOP*.

More problematical is the third question, the categorisation of his early work in terms which are far from aesthetic. Inevitably, given the heterogeneous nature of Machado's work and his varied aesthetic development, critics have attempted to discern specific patterns of evolution while others have insisted on a unity. In the first category is Gicovate (1967); in the second, Cernuda (1957), Gullón (1949) and Zubiría (1955). The omission of some poems in the 1903 edition of *S* (with a 1904 reprint) from the 1907 expanded version, *SGOP*,[4]

---

[1] Soledades (Madrid: Imprenta de A. Álvarez, 1903), with a reprint in 1904 (Madrid: Imprenta de Valero Díaz, 1904) (hereinafter S).
[2] *Soledades. Galerías. Otros poemas*, Biblioteca Hispano-Americana (Madrid: Librería de Pueyo, 1907) (hereinafter *SGOP*).
[3] 'He aquí un poeta solitario y esquivo, que se mantiene siempre alejado del tumulto de las polémicas y de las luchas literarias. Parecía casi que el mundo oficial le ignoraba hasta el momento en que la Academia le acogió en su seno (1927). Y Machado se complacía de esta obscuridad ... "Soledad" es la inspiración de Machado: "Soleda-des" se titulan sus primeras poesías...', Ezio Levi, 'Antonio Machado', *Hispania*, 11, 6 (1928), 471–6 (471).
[4] An excellent analysis of the changes between the two collections can be found in

would suggest that Machado sensed that these early poems of the period 1899–1902 had failed to express his revised and maturer vision following his contact with the *Helios* group. I have argued that many of the ideas set out in *SGOP* reappear in *Campos de Castilla* (Cardwell 1989d). These changes made in *SGOP*, following his protracted contact with the intellectual ferment in Madrid between 1902 (when he returned from his second sojourn in Paris) and April 1907 (when he took up a teaching post in Soria where some of the new poems were composed), reflect his contact with the writers gathered around Juan Ramón Jiménez's review, *Helios*, and the belief that Art might foment a regeneration of the nation (Fogelquist 1955; Paniagua 1964; O'Riordan 1973).

Last, a more vexed and polemical question which has distorted the literary history of the period. For some of the critics favouring an evolution, the poetry up until 1907 has been categorised as *modernista*, the work that follows in 1912, *noventayochista* (related to the year 1898, the year of the *Desastre*, when Spain lost the last of her colonies – principally Cuba and the Philippines – in an unequal war with the United States). Both terms are unhelpful. The first phase is supposedly sentimental, inward-looking, even escapist. A second phase, marked by the first edition of *Campos de Castilla* in 1912, apparently finds Machado concerned with the realities of Spain's decline.[5] Yet these terms are ideological and political rather than aesthetic. *S* and *SGOP* are categorised as *modernista* (new, cosmopolitan, ivory-towered, aesthetic, removed from reality); *Campos de Castilla* and some later poetry are associated with the so-called 'Generation of 1898' and the Disaster of that year. Such a division, also applied to other writers of this period, is a political rather than an aesthetic or critico-literary

---

Dolores Romero López (ed.), *Antonio Machado, Soledades* (Exeter: Exeter University Press, 2006). Given this study I have omitted any detailed analysis of the changes Machado made in *SGOP*. I refer the reader to this analysis and those of Geoffrey Ribbans' editions of *SGOP* (Madrid: Editorial Labor, 1975; Madrid: Cátedra, 1998); of Oreste Macrì, (ed.), *Poesía y prosa*, Tomo III, *Prosa completa* (Madrid: Espasa-Calpe / Fundación Antonio Machado, 1988) (hereinafter *PrC*; and of José-Carlos Mainer, *Antonio Machado. Poesía (*Barcelona: Vicens Vives, 1995), all of which list the alterations Machado made.

[5] See for example José Luis Cano, *De Machado a Bousoño, Ínsula* (Madrid, 1955), pp. 12–13, who notes an 'intimismo trémulo y espiritualmente rico' in *S* by contrast with 'una poesía más objetiva y realista' in *Campos de Castilla*.

distinction. The separation into two opposing categories (*enfrentismo*) began in 1912 with a series of essays by José Martínez Ruiz (Azorín)[6] who invented a supposed 'Generation of 1898'. Azorín was referring to writers who emerged in that year, the year of the *Desastre*. In 1913 he penned four more essays setting out the basic terms on which later critics would build. In the next year Manuel, Antonio Machado's elder brother and poet, contended, once more against all the evidence and for personal reasons, that the work of some writers of his own generation, the *modernistas*, was purely aesthetic and escapist (Celma and Blasco 1981), and that the more 'serious' writers, named by Azorín, were concerned to confront the national crisis of 1898. The fact that both writers had their own agendas and that there is no evidence of any essay or work by the whole generation in the press of the time from 1898 until 1912–13 on the subject of the Disaster (Celma Valero 1991) would confirm that their assertions and later versions of them were, and remain, untenable. At the end of the Civil War in late 1939 this separation of the new *fin de siglo* writers into these two groups (*modernista* and *noventayochista*) was revived for specific ideological reasons. In 1940, as the Nationalists consolidated their power as victors of the Civil War, the cultural and educational establishment came under total political surveillance. The Francoist controlled Real Academia and Ministry of Education imposed clear ideological guidelines on literary production and criticism. At a time of total censorship and rationing of paper, the publication of Ángel Valbuena Prat's massive three-volume *Historia de la literatura española*, significantly accompanied by Manuel Machado's *Omnia Opera Lyrica* (with its poems in honour of Franco) and Alonso Cortés's study of Zorrilla and its celebration of Spain, throne and altar, were clear ideological statements of cultural control. The division of *fin de siglo* Spanish literature into two groups in the *Historia* betrays the presence of a discursive pattern of opposed binaries, one developed to its furthest point in the

---

[6] José Martínez Ruiz, 'Generaciones de escritores', *Obras completas* (Madrid: Aguilar, 1954–63), 1912, IX, 1140–3. This essay was followed in 1913 by four articles: under the title 'La generación de 1898' (1913, II, 900–18). Further references to *Obras completas* of any major author will be to volume and page numbers only, set in the main text. For a discussion of these essays see H. Ramsden, 'The Spanish "Generation of 1898"', reprinted from the *Bulletin of the John Rylands University Library of Manchester*, 56, 2 (1974a), 463–91; 57, 1 (1974), 167–95.

title of Díaz-Plaja's *Modernismo frente a noventa y ocho* of 1951 with all the force of that *frente*.[7] The '98 was categorised as 'varonil', 'robusta', 'sana', 'concienzuda' and, especially, 'castellana' (that is, truly Spanish) while the *modernistas* were marginalised as 'femeninos', 'degenerados', 'neuróticos', 'enfermizos' (note the powerful discourses of sex and medicine overtaking aesthetic criteria) and, above all, anti-national: 'cosmopolita' and 'parisina' (equals foreign and decadent). That is: Generation of 1898 good; *modernismo* bad.[8] This division was taken at face value by virtually all the critics from the 1950s onwards and remains common, in many quarters, until today. More recently this view has been challenged (Cardwell 1991; Mainer and Gracia 1997; Blasco 1981 and 2000). Machado appeared difficult to categorise so *S* and *SGOP* were *modernista*; *Campos* belonged to the more patriotic 'Generation of 1898', despite his clear Republican sympathies and his death in Colliure fleeing from the Nationalists.[9]

In what follows I will challenge the assumption that Machado was 'escapist' and 'ivory-towered', placing him in the ferment of ideas of the *fin de siglo* when he penned the poems which appeared in 1903 and, especially, the new poems of 1903–1907. A part of the above problem

---

[7] Geoffrey Ribbans seems to have been influenced by this division when he remarked that *Campos* marked 'un nuevo concepto de la poesía como actitud espiritual constante, idealista y comunal, en contraste con la confección de dogmas e imágenes brillantes que representa el modernismo': Ribbans, 'Machado and Unamuno', *Bulletin of Hispanic Studies*, XXXIV (1957a), 10–28. Guillermo Díaz-Plaja, *Modernismo frente a noventa y ocho*, Madrid: Espasa-Calpe, 1951.

[8] For an analysis of the question of *enfrentismo* see Cardwell, 'Degeneration, Discourse and Differentiation. Modernismo frente a noventayocho Reconsidered', in *Critical Essays on the Literatures of Spain and Spanish America*, Society for Spanish and Spanish American Studies (Boulder, CO: University Press of Colorado, 1991), pp. 29–46. The terms used in this binary division had been present much earlier in the previous century in the attacks on the so-called *gente joven* by supposedly 'scientific' writers like Cesare Lombroso and Max Nordau. Later, after 1900, other critics took up their pseudo-scientific discourses in an attempt to marginalise the new young writers, including Machado. See for example a typical comment of the time by the influential academician, J. Cejador y Frauca, in 1919: 'un arte decadente y nada juvenil, enfermizo y poco vigoroso', *Historia de la lengua y literatura castellanas* (Madrid: Revista de Archivos, Bibliotecas y Museos, 1919), XII, pp. 83–9, a further echo of the earliest attacks at the end of the previous century.

[9] In a letter to Unamuno dated 16 January 1915 Machado attacked 'la Francia reaccionaria' and compared it with a Republican and libertarian France: 'La otra Francia es de mi familia y aun de mi casa, es la de mi padre y de mi abuelo que ... amaron la Francia de la libertad y el laicismo', *PrC*, p. 1573.

is that critics have tended to study Machado's early work in isolation from the milieu in which he wrote, an assumption fostered by many of the early poems which speak, as does the title of his first work itself, of solitude. There can be no doubt that from the late 1890s onwards there was a renaissance in literary production. Given the false label *modernista* (escapist, ivory-towered) Machado is too often separated from this ferment of new ideas. Thus *SGOP* will be studied in the context of this literary and ideological revival, one which rejected the tenets of the late Restoration period with its ideals of nationalism, patriotism, mercantilism, religion and consoling bourgeois illusions, now called into question by the events of 1898. Machado was deeply involved with the leading figures of his time, witnessed by his dedications to poems in *S* and *SGOP* and the correspondence with major writers (Domènech 2009a, Morales 2000 and Mills 2009) further question the supposed division between *modernistas* and '98. These aspects and studies question the idea of the isolated figure presented in earlier studies. Both before, between and after his two stays in Paris (1899 and 1902) Machado was closely associated with the Madrid *tertulias* of the new literary idealism and its ambitions. From 1902 he published many of the poems separately (which were later to appear in *S* and *SGOP*), the majority in the influential magazine of the new group, *Helios* (1903–04), edited by Juan Ramón Jiménez, and other journals of the new wave. I list these first publications in the Notes to the Poems.

Thus, I argue, one must reject the major arguments for assessing Machado's early work: that *S* and *SGOP* were escapist, sentimental and *modernista* and that Machado was a solitary figure immersed in his own personal concerns. Also, that his work can de divided into *modernista* and *noventayochista*. Quite the opposite. At the same time the poet's own intellectual formation in the bosom of an exceptionally talented family and his formal education in the Institución Libre de Enseñanza has also too often been generally overlooked (Cacho Viu 1962 and 2010). The Institución was one of the intellectual centres of the new reforming zeal of the *gente joven*, the writers of the *fin de siglo* whom Machado knew personally and of whom he formed an integral part. Thus his education, his idealism and the new aesthetic and ideological goals of 1900 came together to produce one of the literary masterpieces of the first decade of the twentieth century. An overview of his intellectual formation and an analysis of the ideals of the period in which the two collections were penned will seek to demonstrate that Machado was very much in the mainstream of the idealism of his age as he slowly assembled the poems which appeared in *S* in 1903 and *SGOP* in 1907.

Machado's intellectual formation

The family

> Muy poco conocidos son los antecedentes familiares de una de las cumbres de nuestra literatura contemporánea. Y, sin embargo, la riqueza personal y la altura intelectual de Antonio Machado no puede aislarse del privilegiado ambiente en que creció y en el que forjó su educación. Pertenecía a una ilustre saga familiar de intelectuales y científicos del XIX español, innovadores en sus respectivos campos.[10]

Thus Encarnación Aguilar in one of the earliest assessments of the poet's grandfather, Antonio Machado y Núñez (1815–96). In a letter to Miguel de Unamuno of 16 January 1915 Machado specifically cited his father and grandfather as seminal influences in his education (Gil Novales 1970, 24–5 and Pérez Ferrero 1947, 29–30). Machado's intellectual history must be traced back to the early years of his grandparents, Machado y Núñez and Cipriana Álvarez de Durán (1827–1902) and the imposing figure of Cipriana's uncle, Agustín Durán (1793–1862), author of a defence of Spain's national theatre in his *Discurso* (1828), the editor of the *Colección de romances castellanos anteriores al siglo XVIII* (1828–32), the *Romancero de romances caballerescos e históricos anteriores al siglo XVIII* of 1832 and the *Romancero general*

---

[10] Encarnación Aguilar (ed.), *Antonio Machado y Núñez: Páginas escogidas* (Sevilla, Serie de Publicaciones del Excmo Ayuntamiento de Sevilla, 1989), p. 13. See also Alberto Gil Novales, *Antonio Machado* (Barcelona, 1970: 'Testigos del siglo XX', núm. 16), p. 19: 'Numerosas notas del espíritu de Machado y Álvarez pasaron a su hijo, y no en la menor el gusto por las coplas populares y el tono sentencioso de buena parte de su literatura'; and Xesús Alonso Montero, 'Antonio Machado y Álvarez ("Demófilo") y la poesía popular gallega', *Ínsula*, 506–7 (1989), 7: 'desde antes de sus primeras lecturas, [los hermanos] son educados en los "textos" cantados o dichos de la poesía popular, estas manifestaciones que Don Antonio Machado y Álvarez, padre de los poetas, recoge, compila, clasifica y nota ... [Los hermanos] asisten al entusiasmo que en Demófilo [el padre] suscitan las musas del pueblo'.

in 1849 with their important prefaces and prologues where he focuses on a 'national spirit' as the key to Spain's regeneration rather than on official political and military 'histories' more pressing solutions. Cipriana shared her uncle's high regard for popular poetry and was a noted painter and collector of folk tales. Of his infancy in Seville, Machado recalls learning to read at her knee from popular verse (*PrC*, 1594), a legacy which colours his early work. In collaboration with her son, Antonio Machado y Álvarez (1846–93), Machado's father, she financed his *Biblioteca de las tradiciones populares* among other ventures in 1884, and was a constant intellectual presence and economic support to the extended family until her death in 1902 when Machado was 27 and *S* was almost complete. Her husband and her son, then, were immersed in popular culture, a legacy passed on to the poet (Domènech 2009b).

To explain this fervent interest we must go back to the first decades of the century to understand the intellectual and ideological aspect of this abiding passion for popular verse and folklore. Cipriana and the three Antonios (and including the poet's brother Manuel) shared a common belief in the integrity of popular culture, one rooted in a belief that Spain's leaders had lost the sense of traditional values, ideals rooted not in politics nor in the false patriotism of a fading empire, rather in values expressed in the people, their culture and especially in popular poetry and its themes, all shaped, they believed, by the unique terrain of Spain's varied topography. A sense of inferiority before more powerful nations in the north and the gradual loss of the Spanish Empire in the early 1800s and down the century, accompanied by the desire for a sense of belonging in society, was widespread in intellectual circles within some European Romantic movements and beyond. This sense was particularly strong in Spain and was to reassert itself once more in almost identical terms at the end of the century with the loss of Cuba in the final Disaster of 1898. In the arts it took the form of a *guerra literaria* against established, and now questionable, national values, especially in the new century (Flitter 1993 and Cardwell 2000a).

Espoused in the early 1800s by the Catholic right wing of Romanticism, fearing that throne and altar were under attack from radical Enlightenment ideas and the impact of the Napoleonic invasion in

1808, the theories set out by the Schlegel brothers in the Vienna lectures from 1808 onwards (influenced by the writings of Herder)[11] were widely accepted and popularised across Europe. In Spain the leading disseminator was Johann Nikolaus Böhl von Faber (Tully 2007; Flitter 1991 and 1992), an arch-conservative polemicist. His belief that the 'soul' of Spain was expressed in its popular culture appears also in the prefaces to Durán's collections as noted above, and soon these ideas had a powerful shaping force of their own, expressed in the conservative literature and criticism of the mid-century by Böhl's daughter Cecilia in her *Cuentos* (1859). In García Gutiérrez's *Discurso* to the Real Academia in 1862 he argued that 'las canciones populares dan a conocer la disposición intelectual de un pueblo', a theme echoed in the next year by Lafuente Alcántara's *Cancionero*. These and other works set the tone for intellectual patterns over the rest of the century (Regueiro 2010). By the 1880s the idea had passed from conservative into liberal circles at the very moment when Machado neared his intellectual maturity. By then the Schlegelian/Herderian construct, now much modified with the impact of evolutionism and determinism (the two Machados Núñez and Álvarez were fervent supporters of Darwin and Spencer), had been espoused by radical dissenting writers, notably in the Institución Libre de Enseñanza under the leadership of Giner de los Ríos, and in the writings of Miguel de Unamuno and Ángel Ganivet, all influential on Machado's thinking. One of the clearest examples of the link between Durán, his grandparents and father is a statement Machado made in 1917 in the second edition of *Campos de Castilla* where he rejected the patriotic and national

---

[11] See I. Berlin, *Vico and Herder: Two Studies in the History of Ideas* (London: Hogarth, 1976). Compare Herder and Durán: Herder: 'We have learned to understand epochs and nations more profoundly through a study of national literatures than through the sad and frustrating path of political and military history. In the latter we scarcely see more than how a nation was governed, and the manner in which it allowed itself to be killed; from the former we learn what were its thoughts, its desires, its longings and pleasures, and in what manner it was led by its teachers and inclinations', quoted in Berlin, p. 43. Durán: 'se ven retratadas, aun mayor que en la historia, las costumbres, las creencias, las supersticiones de nuestros mayores ...; allí se ve también el modo esencial y original de existir propio de aquella sociedad, con los progresos y retrocesos que experimentaba la civilización según las vicisitudes y circunstancias de cada época', in 'Discurso preliminar' to *Romancero de romances caballerescos ...* (Madrid: s.l., 1832), p. xvii. This conception was to be transmitted almost verbatim to the young writers and scholars of the *fin de siglo*.

romance (presumably of the conservative wing of Romanticism and later) and its 'official' history of great victories and powerful kings. Unamuno, in *En torno al casticismo* (1895) (which Machado had read) postulated an alternative to official histories, an *intrahistoria* drawn from the common people and the landscape in which they dwelt. The book inspired Machado's protracted epistolary dialogue with Unamuno from 1901 onwards. Machado, too, sought verses, as with his father, rooted in 'el pueblo que los compuso y ... la tierra donde se cantaron' (*PrC*, 1594): the humble people and their unique geography. Hence his rejection of 'la confección de nuevos romances viejos – caballerescos o moriscos – [que] no fue nunca de mi agrado, y toda simulación de arcaísmos me parece ridícula' (*PrC*, 1594). He is probably referring to the revival of the ballad tradition from the 1840s onwards for a bourgeois readership. This view and interpretation of 'el pueblo' and 'la tierra' formed an essential part of Machado's early intellectual formation, especially with his contact with the literary coteries in Madrid from the late 1890s onwards. Thus a short overview of the work and ideas of his grandparents and his father (the family lived together in an apartment in the Palacio de las Dueñas in Seville (Pineda Novo 1990) and, later, once more, in the Madrid apartment after 1883 until the new century) will demonstrate the unbroken line of an abiding interest in and concern for Spain's cultural and intellectual decline. And, in turn, the profound interest in the poetry of the *pueblo* expressed in traditional measures.

Machado's grandfather, faced with a series of national crises and the failure of any progressive programmes, as with his son Antonio Machado y Álvarez, experienced a profound sense of Spain's decline, spiritual, political, cultural and the recognition of the nation's backwardness, intellectual and scientific (Carr 1966). Their specific vision for Spain and their zeal to stimulate the scientific and cultural education of Spain was underpinned by their publications and the belief in a possible national and spiritual regeneration. Their concern, later shared with the poet himself, lies in the persistent question of how to restore national pride, one shared with the radical intellectuals down the century. But why and how?

As Isaiah Berlin notes, nationalism was an obsessive theme in the nineteenth century. Nationalism, he writes, 'springs, as often as not, from a wounded or outraged sense of human dignity, the desire for recognition ... a struggle for equality with great States, and the claim to survive, grow, be free, be allowed to say their word' (Berlin 1996, 252). Given the political, economic, educational and scientific backwardness of Spain, this sense of inferiority was, arguably, the well-spring for an underlying psychological and intellectual process to discover and articulate a lost and redeeming 'spirit'. It was a common theme among the Machados as it was with other leading intellectual figures associated with them.

Machado's grandfather was a convinced Krausist liberal (see below) and Republican (against the monarchy, the established Church, a corrupt government and the army). Conscious of Spain's backwardness he dedicated his energies to a physical, scientific and intellectual regeneration of his homeland. A founder of the new sciences of anthropology and sociology in Spain in 1869, a year after the abdication of Isabel II and temporary new freedoms, his work is set against the fragmentation of the nation's polity as the forces of cantonalism and federalism were ever present. His response, as a leading politician and university professor in Seville, was to establish a unique, time-resistant identity for Andalucía. This he set out in his *Catalogus methodicus mammalium* of 1869 which was more than a classification of physical types. Overlying the scientific argument he postulated the existence of a distinct racial group belonging to the same natural environment, sharing a common history, possessed of a common ancestry and the same view of reality and a culture with which the group could identify (Jiménez/Agudelo Herrero 1990). His espousal of the theories of Darwin, Haeckel and Spencer gave weight to his thesis but the sub-text was the Schlegelian idea of a time-resistant regional and national 'soul' or 'spirit'. This thesis had its influence on his wife and son who together began work collecting popular traditions.

Antonio Machado y Álvarez was similarly involved in intellectual reforms. He founded the Sociedad El Folk-Lore Andaluz in 1879 (the first folklore society in Spain and modelled on the English society), followed over the next four years by his collection of *cante hondo*. In 1884 he began editing his *Biblioteca de las tradiciones populares*, completing nine volumes prior to his early death in 1893 (Pineda Novo 1991; Baltanás 2006b; Acosta/Vázquez 1990). Despite his early attraction to Positivism (Brotherston 1964) his work expresses the now well-established radical form of the search for a national 'soul' and the recovery of popular traditions, especially in poetry. In an article of 1869 he had argued that there existed an intimate link between collective experience and oral tradition as expressed in popular verse, this artistic form the repository of a time-resistant hidden national identity.[12] By 1879 his search for this 'soul' is evident in his rejection of 'la parte más escogida de la sociedad' (Spain's rulers) for the literature of the 'clases incultas',[13] anticipating Unamuno's distinction of *historia* and *intrahistoria* by 15 years. By 1881 in the final paragraph of his *Colección de cantes flamencos*, an art form to which his sons were *aficionados*, he justified his 'scientific' approach in a rejection of 'un convencionalismo estrecho y artificial' to seek 'grandes y nuevos ideales que hoy se ofrecen al arte'.[14] In 1884 he explored the theme further. With reference to folklore he spoke of 'los fenómenos psicológicos del hombre inculto' (*Bases*, p. 5). By 1885 his espousal of the 'voice' and 'spirit' of the common people (as against Spain's ruling classes and the arbiters of taste) was clear. The Sociedad El Folk-Lore, he wrote, 'tiene por objeto reivindicaciones del derecho del pueblo a ser reconocido como un factor importante de la historia humana, y puesto hoy de manifiesto ante Europa que del seno del pueblo español es de donde han surgido en la hora presente todas las iniciativas.'[15] In these statements we find, as Unamuno, Ganivet and others were to express a decade later, the sense of inferiority before more powerful European nations and the exaltation of the *pueblo* as a consoling centre of confidence and the possible source for national regeneration. Indeed, Machado y Álvarez is a precursor of the idea of a national *intrahistoria*. In his *Bases de El Folk-Lore Español* of 1881 he expressed the view that 'todos los elementos constitutivos del genio, del saber y del idioma patrios, contenidos en la tradición oral [son] materialmente indispensables

---

[12] Antonio Machado y Álvarez, 'Apuntes para un artículo literario', *Revista mensual de filosofía, literatura y ciencias*, I (1869), 116–22 (120).
[13] Antonio Machado y Álvarez, *Bases de El Folk-Lore y Reglamento de El Folk-Lore Andaluz* (Sevilla: Imp. y Lit. de El Poniente, 1881), p. 6.
[14] Antonio Machado y Álvarez, *Colección de Cantes flamencos*. Recogidos y anotados por Demófilo (Sevilla: Imp. y Lit. de El Porvenir, 1881), p. xviii.
[15] Antonio Machado y Álvarez, *Manifiesto a los folkloristas de todas las naciones. El Crucero Iberia* (Sevilla: Álvarez y Cia, 1885), p. 1.

del conocimiento y reconstrucción científica de la historia y la cultura española' (p. 5). This belief in the redemptive power of the *pueblo* and its expression in folklore, traditions and oral verse was passed on to his son and remained in the poet and figured largely in the later Mairena writings. In the 1920s and once again in a time of national crisis, his poet son was to envisage the creation of a new Escuela Popular de Sabiduría Superior on the lines set out by his father in the 1880s.[16] In a lecture in 1937 he expressed views almost identical to his father's, the belief in a national 'soul', the need to listen to the voice of an authentic *pueblo* and study its culture, especially its popular culture expressed in *refranes, coplas* and *cante hondo*.

In 1883 the grandfather was appointed to the Chair of Zoology in the Universidad Central in Madrid and the extended family moved with him from Seville. Here a second related phase of the poet's intellectual formation began, a process which was to reinforce these early ideas. With the contact with the Institución Libre de Enseñanza and later with Unamuno and Jiménez, as Romero López has noted, Machado learned that 'La poesía es observación del pueblo humilde y meditación interna. Sin duda a Antonio Machado le fue grato reencontrarse en su madurez con ideas que se asentaban en los cimientos de su primera educación' (Romero López 2006, 36).

The Institución Libre de Enseñanza

Through personal contacts with the teachers of the Institución, and including their father's Krausist friend Federico de Castro of the University of Seville, the Machado brothers were admitted to this major lay educational centre when the grandfather took up his new post in Madrid. Founded in 1876 by a group of liberal university professors who had been dismissed after the collapse of the first

---

[16] See Enrique Baltanás, 'Los orígenes de la Escuela Popular de Sabiduría Superior: la idea de pueblo en Antonio Machado y Álvarez', in Domènech, *Hoy es siempre* (2006), pp. 11–64. The father's theories, given added weight by Unamuno's *En torno al casticismo*, soon became generally accepted. See for example José María Salaverría among many: 'Para conocer el alma de un pueblo, para sondear en sus sentimientos, prejuicios y estados de ánimo tradicionales, pocos medios existirán tan directos y eficaces como el refranero, ese centón de filosofía anónima en que la conciencia popular deja lo íntimo de su ser', *Vieja España* (Madrid, 1907), p. 87. For an excellent overview see H. Ramsden, *The 1898 Movement in Spain* (Manchester: Manchester University Press, 1974b), pp. 155–72.

Republic in 1874 and headed by Francisco Giner de los Ríos, the Institución was the only truly secular educational centre in Spain at the time. It offered a wide liberal curriculum for the free flow of modern ideas freed from the dogmas of Church, Army and State. It was also the home of Krausism, a philosophy imported to Spain from Germany by Sanz del Río and adapted in the 1840s, one soon taken up by a large number of free-thinking intellectuals (López Morillas 1981; DuPont 2013), including Giner (Lipp 1985) and Machado's father (López Álvarez 1996). The Institución, in tune with its Krausist origins, stressed morality in personal and public life, a basic humanism combining a love of science, aesthetics, nature and sport. In essence it was an evangelising message calling on spiritual, aesthetic and evolutionist values. The many moving tributes to Giner on his death in 1915, including one by Machado himself on 21 February 1915 (*PrC*, 1575–7), are a token of the high esteem and affection many young writers felt for a man whose conduct and personal example continued to inspire them. So, too, to the Krausist spirit, an attitude of mind and outlook, which underpinned the school and its leader, Giner. Azorín, soon to be a central figure in the new movement, observed that 'El krausismo, a nuestro entender, no es una filosofía sino una moral, y en eso estaba su fuerza considerable.'[17] Giner rejected 'lo aparatoso, lo decorativo ... que acompaña a las cosas del espíritu'; his example was never one of a rejection of the world, 'contemplativo y extático', rather 'laborioso y activo'. His aim was to 'hacer hombres ... hombres bien equilibrados, de temperamento ideal, de amor a las grandes cosas'. But their example was not to be imposed from above as with the Church-dominated system of education in partnership with the State and the Army, the product of 'condiciones históricas'. Rather the new 'movimientos ideales' were to be founded 'en las profundidades del espíritu del tiempo' (the *alma nacional*), only to be realised

---

[17] José Martínez Ruiz (Azorín), 'Don Julián Sanz del Río', in *Dicho y hecho* (Madrid: Clásicos Castellanos, 1957), pp. 109–10 and, in his 'invention' of the 'Generation of 1898' set out in his 1913 articles (see note 6), he cites the impact of the Krausist Institución Libre de Enseñanza in the awakening of idealism in the new generation (II, 900–18). Unamuno voiced a similar view in 1903: 'Pocos movimientos espirituales han sido más fecundos y beneficiosos en España que el que provocó y fomentó aquel bienhadado krausismo': Unamuno, *Obras completas* (Madrid: Afrodisio Aguado, 1958) (hereinafter *O.C.*), III, 592.

'mediante una preparación que podría decirse profesional y laboriosa' (López Morrillas 1969, 116).[18] This was a slow process, attentive to the latent pulse of history, an outlook related to the determinist 'intrahistoric' idealism set out above, one expressed in an art that was drawn from the people and which spoke to them. Giner, too, shared the view that a study of the people and its culture offered a way to reform and a rediscovery of the national 'soul'.[19] The initial step was to prepare oneself spiritually (a form of lay religion) to make one's life an example for others, what Sanz del Río (the Krausist father of the movement and adapter of Krause's philosophy) and Darío, later, termed a 'sacerdocio espiritual'. Thus Sanz: 'Elevado a este sacerdocio espiritual ... será nuestro primer deber enseñar la verdad, propagarla y vivir enteramente para ella.'[20] Giner echoes his master: 'Será nuestro primer deber enseñar la verdad, propagarla y vivir enteramente para ella', given that 'esta acción ... puede estimular en un individuo la reforma interior de otros ... la elevación de las almas'.[21] The process, Giner continued, as Unamuno was also to argue, would begin with a few inspired men. 'Es ley que todo despertamiento se inicie siempre en una minoría' (XVII, p. 150). In the new century Jiménez spoke of 'una inmensa minoría' and Ortega of 'los mejores'. Machado, as we shall see, was to echo Giner's condemnation of a 'demagogía de vientre' (gut demagogy), as was Jiménez, Machado's friend, in his own condemnation of a

---

[18] Giner's messianism inspired Jiménez's *Helios* review in which Machado placed several of his poems. Jiménez wrote to Rubén Darío in 1903 to say that *Helios* was to serve as 'un alimento espiritual'. The Manifesto of *Helios* opposed 'una fuerza negativa ... y propugna las fuerzas positivas de la educación y la cultura'. Indeed, the magazine saw itself as declaredly and militantly evangelising: 'paladines de nuestra muy amada Belleza, prontos a reñir cien batallas del verbo y de espíritu. ¡Guárdanos tú, la Dilectísima, por quien osamos entrar en lid!'. These statements echo almost exactly those of Salas y Quiroga, Pastor Díaz and Gil y Carrasco in the 1830s and 1840s but now with a decided emphasis on a 'war', the *guerra literaria* centred on *Helios*.

[19] Francisco Giner de los Ríos, echoing Herder and Durán, 'Estúdiese aquélla (la literatura de un pueblo) y los más remotos tiempos y las generaciones más olvidadas nos prestarán con toda la pompa de sus grandezas, con todas sus miserias, con todas sus aspiraciones, con todos sus extravíos', Giner de los Ríos, 'Consideraciones sobre el desarrollo de la literatura moderna', *Ensayos* (Madrid: Alianza, 1969), p. 54.

[20] Julián Sanz del Río, 'Discursos pronunciados en la Universidad Central en la solemne inauguración del año académico de 1857 a 1858', in *Ideal de la humanidad para la vida*, 2nd edn (Madrid: Rivadenyra, 1871), pp. 344–5.

[21] Francisco Giner de los Ríos, *Obras completas* (Madrid: Pueyo, 1916–1936), II, 8. All intercalated references by volume and page are to this edition.

'sociedad soez' (obscene society) in one of his earliest essays.[22] Giner's emphasis was on a slow but irresistible programme of social regeneration by select individuals who would energise their fellow men by their example always in tune with the 'spirit' or 'soul' of the nation as read through a study of the *pueblo* and its culture. This minority group would offer an alternative to the values of a bourgeois Restoration society creating a semi-religious élite who embodied 'ese espíritu educador que remueve, como la fe, los montes, y que lleva en sus senos, quizá cual ningún otro, el porvenir del individuo y de la patria' (*Ensayos*, p. 115). On another occasion Giner noted that 'nuestro objetivo en el mundo no debe ser gobernar mejor, ni ser mejor gobernados, sino simplemente ser mejores' (*Ensayos*, p. 78), a sentiment Jiménez repeats in 'Rejas de oro' in 1900 and Machado, as we shall see, takes up again in a letter to Jiménez in 1903. In these statements we note the language of a lay evangelism (note the repeated use of the language of religion) as much as evolutionism, both of which appear in the writings of the radical intellectuals of the time (Flitter 1993). This, then, was the tenor of Machado's education in the Institución, an outlook and a messianic programme which he was to express in his work and which was to shape his early collections when he returned from Paris in 1902 and joined the *Helios* group (Casalduero 1964; Heydl Cortínez 1995; Cardwell 2006; Romero López, 2006, 35–7). Art and Beauty with a necessary ethical message drawn from the probing of one's own spiritual doubts and hopes, expressed in literature and in tune with Giner's and the Institución's message, would be the battleground of these evangelical new writers.

Paris and Symbolism
In July 1899 Machado and his brother poet Manuel, given the economic straits of the family fortunes following the death of their grandfather in 1893 and the early death of their father in 1896, went to Paris as translators at the Garnier publishing house. There the two devoted themselves to the bohemian and artistic fringes of Parisian cultural life and imbibed the current literary fashion of Symbolism,

---

[22] Juan Ramón Jiménez, 'Rejas de oro' (1900), in *Libros de prosa* (Madrid: Aguilar, 1969), p. 214, and the poem '¿A varios amigos? where the poet is even more caustic about Spanish bourgeois society, a theme Machado reiterates, as we shall see, in a letter to Jiménez in 1903.

notably the poetry of Paul Verlaine and Stéphane Mallarmé, whom Machado met, and who – as Geoffrey Ribbans (1957b, 1968/69, 1971, 1976/77, 1979), Paul Ilie (1962) and Rafael Ferreres (1975, 129–54) have shown – was, among others, to prove influential, if carefully disguised, in the composition of *S* and *SGOP*. The impact of these years has been documented in considerable detail in Aguirre's seminal study of the considerable presence of French and Belgian Symbolist writers in Machado's oeuvre (Aguirre 1973; see also Gómez Montero 1990; Grass and Risley 1979; Alarcón Sierra 2009). After his return in 1900 he published his first poems in the radical review *Electra* in 1901, followed by many more in other progressive reviews and subsequently collected in *SGOP* (see my Notes to the Poems). In 1902, with the death of his grandmother and more straitened circumstances,[23] Machado, with the help of the Guatemalan diplomat and writer Enrique Gómez Carrillo, obtained a post at the Guatemalan embassy in Paris but returned at the end of the year when he submitted *S* to the printers. The volume appeared early the next year bearing all the marks in its style of his cultural experiences in Paris and his early education. By 1902 Symbolism as a poetic style was well established, as was its cousin the Decadence, from which influence the poet was not immune (Cardwell 1974; 2000c).

The influence of French and Belgian Symbolism on Machado is indisputable (Aguirre 1973). Machado's friend Emilio Carrère noted in 1905, in the 'Nota' to his *Florilegio de rimas modernas* (Madrid: Pueyo, p. 7), that Machado was 'el grave sacerdote del simbolismo', suggesting that by then the poet's verses were seen as Symbolist. Many echoes, themes and Symbolist practices are evident in the two collections of 1903 and 1907. But how does Symbolism manifest itself as a poetic practice? In the Appendix, I offer a critical reading of a typical Symbolist-influenced poem. The reading offered attempts to show how Symbolism works at the creative rather than the intellectual and symbolic level. Beginning with the world of 'dream' and/or 'memory',

---

[23] See Jiménez's comments on the Machado family at this time: 'Madrid. Abuela queda viuda y regala la casa. Madre inútil. Todos viven pequeña renta abuela. Casa desmantelada. Familia empeña muebles. No trabajan, ya hombres. Casa de la picaresca. Venta de libros viejos. Muere abuela', Jiménez, *El modernismo. Notas de un curso (1953)* (Mexico: Aguilar, 1962), pp. 159–60. See also M. Pérez Ferrero, *Vida de Antonio Machado y Manuel* (Madrid: Rialp, 1947).

a form of special consciousness, provoked by a real incident or specific landscape (often a closed garden or plaza), Machado seeks an adequate form of expression, a symbol. As he wrote in 'La fuente' from *S* (not repeated in *SGOP* perhaps since it was too direct): 'Y doquiera que me halle, en mi memoria, / – sin que mis pasos a la fuente guíe – / el símbolo enigmático aparece ...', a theme he repeats in 'Crepúsculo' (again omitted from *SGOP)*: 'Roja nostalgia el corazón sentía, / sueños bermejos, que en el alma brotan / de lo inmenso consciente, / cual de región caótica y sombría ...'. The ellision of dream and the colour 'bermejo' here, always associated with golden fruit in *SGOP*, refers to the Greek belief that the home of the Muses stood in the Golden Woods of Helicon and the inspiring spring of Hippocrene near Mount Parnassus, a motif which the poet employs again and again in *SGOP*. In terms of practice Machado employs a language of suggestion following Mallarmé's dictum that the poet should 'suggérer, ... évoquer petit à petit un objet pour montrer un état d'âme, ou, inversement, choisir un objet et en dégager un état d'âme, par une série de déchiffrements' (suggest, ... evoke an object little by little to show a state of soul or, in another way, choose an object and draw out a state of soul by a series of decipherings).[24] To realise what Mallarmé, in the same article, termed 'le rêve' (the dream), the result of 'suggestion', the poet would discover the 'symbol': 'C'est l'usage parfait de ce mystère qui constitue le symbole' (869) (It is the perfect use of this mystery which constitutes the symbol). Thus, Machado suggests; moods created from meditations set in closed spaces, galleries, at times from windows, or set before distant horizons lead to his symbolic creations (Gullón 1958). That is, the poem is created from a series of receding 'frames', one giving way inwards or outwards to another, or of distorting mirrors reflecting multiple prismatic images (Cardwell 1985a, 1987, 1989a, 1989b, 1990, 1997a; Meyers 1954; Zardoya 1961; Ruiz Ramón 1962a). The poet meditates on time and passing time; he seeks to detain a fleeting form or shadow leading to a hidden source or meaning, one often religious, even mystical in tone, as we shall see in the Notes. He probes dreams, visions and, above all, memory – memories of childhood and meditations on life, passing

---

[24] Stéphane Mallarmé, '"Sur L'Evolution Littéraire" (Enquête de Jules Huret)', *Oeuvres complètes* (Paris: Éditions Gallimard, 1945), p. 869.

time, expressed in rivers, fountains, autumn, fallen leaves and sunsets, and the role of the artist himself in giving these thoughts substance (Ribbans 1972). He considers the act of poetic creation, questioning his art with the ever-present fear of the loss of inspiration and authenticity. In many poems he sustains a mono-dialogue where he seeks reassurance that his inspiration has not failed him and that his poetic journey of illumination is not merely a mirage, an image distorted in a series of mirrors or self-reflecting spaces. At other times he casts himself as a poor player on a stage, a failed actor who spouts grotesque lines; at others he compares the past and present: 'Poeta ayer, hoy triste y pobre / filósofo trasnochado, / tengo en monedas de cobre / el oro de ayer cambiado' (XCV. See also XCI). The poems employ sets of tropes which underpin the expression of these aspects: the use of symbolic images, often traditional, popular or classical figures and spaces (these latter owing to the influence of his cultural upbringing by his grandmother and father): enclosed gardens, walled patios, tiny squares, avenues, hidden paths; symbolic forms – lemons, golden fruit, golden light, fleeting shadows, fountains, sometimes classical symbolic forms (nymphs, the huntress), at others religious references taken from Spain's mystical writers, an aspect to which I shall return. In a sense Machado attempts to create a paradise at the end of his search, a version of the pastoral tradition of the Golden Age (Oringer 2001). Arguably unique to Machado is the use of an internal world, his 'galerías' which become disturbing as they mutate into 'criptas hondas', labyrinths and halls of prismatic glass which reflect myriad and disturbing images.[25] The employment of these motifs through a poetry of nuance and diffused expression often operates on more than one level, moving from a known reality to the expression of a personal truth or to an evocation of the national 'soul' which is related to the search for 'self'. Thus, beneath the more obvious evidence of Symbolist practice lies an aspect related to Machado's intellectual formation: the search for a national, time-resistant 'soul' and the concomitant search for 'self'. Machado often combines an allusive style with echoes of popular verse in an attempt to express, in a modern idiom, the voice

---

[25] Later, in the 1920s, Ramón del Valle-Inclán was to depict Spanish society in the distorting mirrors set in the Callejón del Gato, a street in Madrid. Perhaps Machado had seen the same mirrors.

of the *pueblo*. But that style, too, represented a search for a personal faith, as we shall see below.

The search for the 'soul' of the *pueblo* in its landscape and literature

The search for the national 'soul' had begun in the early nineteenth century in Spain's Romantic Movement. By the mid-century that search had become a commonplace (Regueiro 2010). The poet Gustavo Adolfo Bécquer, much admired by Machado and his contemporaries for his allusive and popular style in his *Rimas* and *Leyendas* (published posthumously in 1871), was influenced by Augusto Ferrán's *La soledad* (1861) (anticipating Machado's title). A diplomat in Berlin, Ferrán's theories were shaped by the dominant interest in the *Volksgeist* of Herder and the Schlegel brothers, which idea, now applied to popular poetry and folktales, appears in Bécquer's *Leyendas* and, especially, in *Historia de los templos de España* (1857). By the 1880s there emerged a consistent academic interest in collecting popular verse, the philosophical and pseudo-scientific interest in defining Spain's unique 'alma' and a desire to express the authentic voice of its people in popular verse measures. In Seville in the late century the Machado family and their friends and critic-poets, Rodríguez Marín and Montoto y Rautenstrauch, in Málaga poets like Narciso Díaz de Escovar and José Sánchez Rodríguez; in Murcia, Ricardo Gil; in Almería Durbán Orozco and Arturo Reyes, also began to pen verses based on popular themes and on traditional metrical forms. One of the foremost scholars of Spanish folklore and popular verse after Machado's father was Ramón Menéndez Pidal (1866–1951) who took up the Chair of Romance Studies in the University of Madrid in 1899 and made acquaintance with the new poets. He soon became a powerful exponent of the roots of popular verse and its lost connections with the past to define a national 'pyschology': 'la condición psicológica uniforme [de España] depende de la conformidad del carácter apartadizo ibérico'[26] (Iberian unsociability). In the same year Rafael Altamira, a scholar associated with the Institución

---

[26] R. Menéndez Pidal, *Discursos leídos ante la Real Academia Española en la recepción pública de D. Ramón Menéndez Pidal el 19 de octubre de 1902* (Madrid: Establecimiento Tipográfico de la Viuda e Hijos de M. Tello, 1902), p. 12.

and close friend of Giner and Azorín, wrote in 1902, in the revealingly entitled *Psicología del pueblo español*, of an 'historia integral' and the need to study 'las notas constantes que, en medio de la variedad enorme de los distintos tiempos hasta hoy, presenta nuestro pueblo',[27] by which he included a study of popular verse. By the beginning of the new century such interpretations among Machado's group was a commonplace (Cardwell 1981 and 1984a; Ramsden 1974b). This was accompanied by a rise in *flamenco* clubs and folklore societies to which former the Machado brothers were fervent adherents. All these activities and responses bear witness to the original German Romantic passion for the re-discovery and the cataloguing of unsophisticated cultures combined with later theories of evolution and determinism. Azorín, ever sensitive to changing aesthetic fashions, made clear this shift from a Restoration rhetoric based on history and national conservative ideals to a new voice expressing the more authentic life of the ordinary humble people:

> ¿Cómo no iban a reaccionar los escritores de 1898 contra el énfasis, el superlativo elogioso y la hipérbole desmandada? [the overstated historical emphasis of the preceding generation] ... Pero había otra causa de discrepancia. En este asunto encontramos lo verdaderamente esencial. De la historia pasamos a la estética en general. No se trata ya nuevamente de escribir la historia, sino de ver la vida ... Los grandes hechos son una cosa y los menudos hechos son otra. Se historian los primeros, se desdeñan los segundos. Y los segundos forman la sutil trama de la vida cotidiana ... Ahí radica la diferencia estética del 98 con relación a lo anterior ... Lo que no se historiaba, ni novelaba, ni se cantaba en la poesía, es lo que la generación del 98 quiere historiar, novelar y cantar. (VI, 232)

Ignoring the use of the term 'the writers of 1898' which, as we have seen, is a personal invention of Azorín, this statement is, in essence, a reiteration of Herder, the Schlegels, the Spanish Romantics and Unamuno's celebrated distinction between *historia* and *intrahistoria* set out in *En torno al casticismo* (1893–96). This discrimination soon became accepted among the young *gente nueva*. Yet Machado's father had expressed the same search, nearly thirty years before, for what Unamuno was later to term 'la tradición eterna [que] no se encontraría

---

[27] Rafael Altamira, *Psicología de nuestro pueblo* (Barcelona: Antonio López, 1902), p. 60.

en libros y papeles' and 'la sustancia del progreso' (II, 73). '¿Queréis conocer la historia de un pueblo? Ved sus romances', wrote Machado y Álvarez in 1884. '¿Aspiráis a saber lo que es capaz? Estudiad sus cantares.'[28] Between the labours of his father and the correspondence with Unamuno at the time of the composition of *S*, sensitive to the new form of thinking of his generation, Machado's verses lie at the centre of this finisecular idealism and search for new forms. From Böhl von Faber and Durán onwards into the new twentieth century writers and intellectuals sought to find the 'alma popular' latent in the common people and its culture, whatever their political colour. By the new century the idea was a 'given'. Indeed, in 1899 the Granadan writer, Nicolás María López, had published a set of prose poems under the title *Tristeza andaluza*.[29] In the following year the Malagan poet José Sánchez Rodríguez published his *Alma andaluza* (Sánchez Trigueros/Cardwell 1996). In 1903 the critic José Nogales, under the title 'Alma andaluza', published in Azorín's journal, *Alma Española* (I, núm. 5, 6-XII-1903), drew attention to the effect of the 'medio físico' and its correspondent effect on people (a clear reference to the determinist-guided theory of a national 'soul'). Nogales, a keen observer of the new trends, like many others of this period, was likewise seeking to define 'el carácter andaluz'. Among various characteristics he suggested 'inercia, pasividad, desconfianza' as salient features and, especially, an obsession with melancholia and death which he found richly expressed in Andalucía's 'arte popular'. To this he added that 'el *alma andaluza* es una gran alma dormida que sueña ... No sé con qué'; hence a sense of mystery and enigma. He might have been writing of Machado's *S*. In *Tierras solares*, in the next year, Rubén Darío, in the essay 'Málaga', lamented the effects of industrial progress in the city and the new and false commercial culture of 'pandereta, navaja, mantón y calañés' (tambourine, dagger, shawl and flamenco hat),[30] a Romantic and exotic view promulgated over eighty years before by French writers like Gautier, Hugo and D'Amicis. *Cante flamenco* (the Machado brothers

---

[28] Antonio Machado y Álvarez, 'Introducción al estudio de las canciones populares', *Estudios sobre literatura popular*, 1a Parte (Madrid: Fernando Fe, 1884), p. 6.
[29] Nicolás María López, *Tristeza andaluza* (Granada: Tip. Lit. De la Viuda e Hijo de Sabatel, 1899); Facsimile edn (Granada, Editorial Comares, 1988).
[30] Rubén Darío, *Tierras solares, Obras completas* (Madrid: Afrodisio Aguado, 1950), III, 859. Hereinafter references are to this edition.

were keen adherents), he noted, had lost its roots, 'sus antiguos bríos' (its ancient verve), but its genuine content, the *copla*, expresses the real 'soul' in its expression of love and death. In his review of Jiménez's *Arias tristes* (1903), 'La tristeza andaluza' (III, 829–93), Darío returned to the theme of *cante hondo* to argue that the *cantaor* 'ha recogido el alma triste de la España mora ... Más que una pena personal, es una pena nacional'. Jiménez sings 'toda la inmensa tristeza que hay en la tierra andaluza' and Manuel Machado's *Alma* of 1900 had already explored this popular vein (Cardwell 1989c). This, he argues, is very different from the French Romanticised vision and the then popular illustrations of *cante hondo* on publicity bills and boxes of dates and matches. For this reason Jiménez's sad verses mark 'un poeta completamente de su tierra'. Thus, for Darío, Jiménez is a product of his environment, 'andaluz de la triste Andalucía. Es de los que cantan la verdad de su existencia y claman el secreto de su ilusión'. He expresses 'las mismas visiones y las mismas ansias que ... las coplas populares' (III, 896). That is, sadness, doubts, lost illusions, the emotions this generation had diagnosed in the national character, especially Andalusian character, are those which Machado as a *sevillano* will express. At the same time Darío praises Jiménez's Symbolist style.

By the new century, then, there existed a convergence of themes among the young poets of which Machado formed an integral part: the search for an expression of a national or regional 'soul'; the expression of personal sadness and a meditation on death and decay expressed in popular verse forms yet in the new Symbolist style. This was accompanied by an evangelical desire, through their art, to 'redeem' and 'regenerate' the nation and its popular culture. The sadness of the poet is both an expression of that of his homeland as much as his own. Indeed, sadness is sought as a well-spring of inspiration as Jiménez noted in a review of Martínez Ruiz's (Azorín) *Antonio Azorín* in 1903: 'porque de esa maldita tristeza española, de esa melancolía de nuestra raza, de que se habla Martínez Ruiz, a mí me ha correspondido una buena parte, a mí que he nacido en uno de esos pueblos tan opacos, tan sedentarios, tan melancólicos' (*Libros de prosa*, p. 233). In this statement, an echo of the style of Azorín himself, where personal concerns push reality aside, we see confirmed the union of the general melancholia of *fin de siglo* letters and the determinist search for a 'soul' ('nuestra raza') to be found in Spain's countryside and in its popular literature. The added effect is Symbolism where personal emotions are imposed upon place and objects. It is not surprising, then, that Manuel Machado included a section of 'Cantares' in his *Alma* of 1900, and that Jiménez published his *Arias tristes* three years later in *romance* measure, the same year that Machado published his own doubts, melancholia and glosses on popular themes and verses.

Machado's use of popular tradition

If we examine the prosody of Machado's early collections, of the ninety-six poems of *SGOP* only seven employ an Italianate or Spanish Golden Age measure, the *serventesio*.[31] The rest are in *romance* (the most traditional of popular measures or variations on that measure), *redondillas* (again a traditional form), the *silva-romance* (the naturalisation of an Italian form and by 1800 traditional), and measures from genuine popular culture with echoes of *flamenco*, the *copla* and the *soleá*. Thus, in tune with contemporary writers, Machado, too, elects to write in a popular and traditional mode, one eschewing the more learned and Italianate forms, one which echoes the 'voice' of the people (Predmore 1989; Gutiérrez Carbajo 2006). In the same way, the themes of many of Machado's verses belong to popular tradition while expressed in the modern Symbolist and renovated 'popular' style. Like many of his contemporaries he revives the image of the garden or orchard as a place for love or meditation, fountains (Alonso 1965), the motif of roads and paths, themes from *cante hondo* and the *copla*, love and lost love, and death. It goes without saying that, later, in the Mairena musings, Machado returned again and again to the theme of folklore, popular verse and song as abiding elements and as a guide for the future. 'Se desarrolló un punto de vista en el que, mediante el estudio de la cultura y las tradiciones, el hombre pudiera encontrar y sintonizar su propio espíritu con el espíritu de su cultura latente' (Cardwell 1994, 87). The humble *pueblo*, Mairena argued, 'sabe más, y sobre todo, mejor que nosotros ... Es muy posible que, entre nosotros, el saber universitario no puede competir con el folklore, con el saber

---

[31] 11-syllable lines in quatrains with consonantal rhyme abaab, etc. See poems XV, XVII, XX, XXXV, XLIX, LXXXIV and XCIV.

popular'. That is, the supposedly well-educated bourgeoisie and the landed aristocracy claim to know more than the humble artisan. Yet, 'de un pueblo inteligente, fino, sensible ...había mucho que aprender... para poder luego enseñar bien a las clases adineradas'.[32]

The search for Spain: time and passing time

The search for a timeless past expressed in popular measures, then, is a marked theme in the early collections. In poem X, for example, Machado creates a picture common in the work of his *tertulia* friends and painters, the silent decaying towns of Spain, a mirror to their sense of lost illusions (Ramsden 1974a and 1974b; Cardwell 1981 and 2012). The second part of the poem, shaped, arguably, by Bécquer's 'Tres fechas' with its fleeting face at a window, points in another direction; the search for an ideal. In the following poem XI, he echoes, amid a dreamlike evocation of the landscape or, rather, a 'moodscape', the lamentations which accompany the traditional *pasos* bearing the Virgin Mary, witnessed in childhood in Seville. In poem VIII, written in 1899 and in *romancillo*, he evokes a timeless past where the voices of children and songs are intertwined with the flow of fountains uniting past and present in a scene filled with melancholy at the passing of time and loves past. The flowing of fountains and rivers, images of the inexorable flow of time, form a substrate of these poems. He expands on the theme of time's passing in poem LXVI, here expressed in the music of the *bordón*, a single string instrument in *cante popular* (and also a support or guide) which accompanies the *cantaor*, transformed into an expression of pain (the *pena* of *cante hondo*) – 'la negra nota de angustia' – where dreams of the past fade into an ellipsis, a sigh. In another poem (XIX), again in *romancillo*, he returns to the fountain image to evoke the timeless figure of the woman at the well, the 'linda doncellita' filling her urn and, in her task, she is heedless of the poet, for she is timeless. Flowing water in rivers and fountains, like the flow of time, is both constant and, yet, ever-changing. Yet, on one occasion,

---

[32] Antonio Machado, *Obras completas* (Mexico: Editorial Séneca, 1940), pp. 500–1. For a fuller discussion see Paulo de Carvalho-Neto, *La influencia del folklore en Antonio Machado* (Madrid: Ediciones Demófilo, 1975) and Manuel Urbano, *El cante jondo en Antonio Machado* (Madrid: Ediciones Demófilo, 1982).

Machado caricatures the theme of the popular *cante*. 'Fantasía de una noche de abril' (LII) is a rare example of a pastiche on his own style and that of his fellow poets, even Espronceda's *El estudiante de Salamanca* (1838–40), through echoes of their and his own verses.[33]

Machado and his contemporaries: shared ideals and obsessions

In 1898 Spain lost the last vestiges of her empire with the twin naval defeats in Cuba and the Philippines. Conservatives, Liberals and Republicans all blamed one another; the armed forces blamed the Government, they blamed the forces. Pablo Iglesias, leader of the Socialists (whom Machado admired) wrote in *El Liberal* on 4 October 1898 on the failure of 'todos, políticos, militares, administradores'. The young writers, while expressing their loss of faith in their rulers, Spain's traditional ideals and the nation itself, began to seek some form of faith in the hidden qualities of the hitherto marginalised *pueblo*.[34] This process, of course, is in tune with the intellectual processes and similar political crises we have traced from the German Historical School, the Spanish Romantics and the Krausists of the Institución. Indeed, commentarists perceived a schism between those who had failed the nation and the new generation.[35] In his *La crisis intelectual del 98*, E. Inman Fox presented a picture of the young men of the so-called '98 (in reality the young generation of middle-class writers who emerged at the turn of the century, including Machado) torn between a profound scepticism and Spain's capacity for change in political and moral conditions. They sought, he argued,

---

[33] This will explain G.W. Ribbans' comment in the 'Prólogo' to *SGOP* (1975), that 'Fantasía ...' is a 'poesía narrativa [que] representa un esfuerzo de evocación de su nativa Andalucía ... poco frecuente en él', p. 22. It is an isolated poem simply because it is a pastiche.

[34] See for example Unamuno: 'Después del desastre colonial ha entrado en España a no pocos escritores cierta comezón por el estudio de la psicología de nuestro pueblo o de nuestros pueblos' (1902: III, 715). For further details see Ramsden 1974a, pp. 1–3 and 46–9.

[35] See, for example, one comment among many: 'Están los *intelectuales* españoles irremisiblemente separados en dos ramas: *modernistas*, que significa tanto como espíritus expansivos abiertos a todas las corrientes científicas y artísticas, y otros varones que yo llamo *anticuados*, por no denominar con adjetivo más fuerte y gráfico', Camilo Bargiela, *Luciérnagas (Cuentos y sensaciones)* (Madrid: 1900), pp. i–xxv ('Modernistas y anticuados').

an energetic, even evangelical, idealism concerning the national future, 'el radical vaivén (to and fro) entre la violenta protesta y la huida hacia la meditación metafísica' (Fox 1976, 226. See also Blanco Aguinaga 1970, Ramsden 1974a, 67–95; Mainer 1974 and Mainer/Gracia 1997). But the protest in the group gathered around Jiménez, Machado and the *Helios* magazine was far from violent; quite the reverse. Their campaign, as *Helios* announced, was to be with words, with their art. While their crisis was rooted in a sense of impotence and failing beliefs in the patriotic and militaristic pronouncements of the governing and mercantile classes,[36] these men did not turn to political or social action. The emphasis was, as we have seen, a psychological one and a search for the national 'soul', especially in its varied landscape, its literature and popular poetic culture. As early as 1899 in a review of Villaespesa's *La copa del rey de Thule*, the young Jiménez spoke of an 'empuje juvenil' (youthful thrust) in poetry and art. Villaespesa, in turn, in the prologue to Jiménez's *Almas de violeta* (1900) wrote: 'Las modernas tendencias literarias atraen cada día mayor números de espíritus entusiastas, y aunque no faltan voluntades mezquinas (poor-spirited) ..., la mayoría de la *Juventud*, la Juventud batalladora y fecunda, se agrupa en torno a *la nueva bandera*, decidida a emprender la conquista del "Ideal"'. But that 'empuje' and that warlike spirit (note the terms employed which Machado takes up in poem LXI), the real meaning of the *guerra literaria,* was soon to be a common theme as the correspondence between Jiménez and his artistic 'hermano' Machado shows.[37] When, in his magazine *Helios* in

---

[36] Their reaction became a commonplace. See for example Rubén Darío in *Los raros* (1896) where the idealist artist is destroyed by 'tenderos, rentistas o merchifles. ... La ciencia impide al poeta penetrar y tender las alas el la atmósfera de las verdades ideales'; José Enrique Rodó's *Ariel* (1900): 'el sentido de la utilidad material y el bienestar [son] particularmente funestos a la difusión de preocupaciones puramente ideales'; Miguel de Unamuno: 'Maldito lo que se gana con un progreso que nos obliga a emborracharnos con el negocio, con el trabajo y la ciencia, para no oír la voz de la sabiduría eterna' 'La vida es sueño', November 1898, in Unamuno, *O.C.*, III, 407–17. See also Ernesto Bark: 'La brutal y despiadada metalización, característico de estos tiempos, ha provocado una verdadera sed de ideales, una pasión por lo noble y etéreo', *La santa bohemia* (Madrid: Biblioteca Germinal, Editorial Coop. H. de Autores, 1913), p. 16. For Machado's response see Michael P. Predmore, 'The Vision of an Imprisoned and Moribund Society in the *Soledades, Galerías y otros poemas* [sic] of Antonio Machado', *Ideologies and Literature*, II, 8 (1978), 14–30.

[37] This correspondence is included in *PrC* and, with a commentary in R. Gullón,

November 1903, the former wrote 'hoy, más que nunca, tenemos una juventud que quiere trabajar' (*Libros de prosa*, pp. 208, 250), Jiménez was drawing attention to a process which had begun some four or five years before. The new language was one of war, but it was to be a war of words, of idealistic art. For the English Romantics, as Brian Goldberg (2007) has shown, poetry was socially useful, but its utility and effectiveness in this field of influence depended significantly on an acknowledgement of the professional status of the poet. The poet, thus, and his professional judgement, controls the taste and aesthetics of the readership. It is the poet's task to ascertain his duty rather than responding to the dictates of the marketplace. Poetry is, therefore, educative and cultural. The influence of Shelley, especially, and his *Defence of Poetry* (1840), as we shall see, was to prove seminal among the writers of the *Helios* group (Young 1980; González/Rodríguez/Cardwell 2008).

Informing this desire for a spiritual, moral and aesthetic revolution lay the Krausist ethic of the Institución and the presence of Giner de los Ríos who attended many of the tertulias in which Jiménez and Machado moved. As Inman Fox correctly observes, 'a pesar de que indicios de que no todos los escritores del 98 [properly *fin de siglo*] estaban familiarizados con los principios específicos del krausismo, no hay duda de que se educaron dentro de un ambiente intelectual imbuídos por ellos' (94). The pursuit of Beauty in Art included notions of Goodness and Truth. This idea, of course, echoed the reading of Shelley in the new century. As early as 1870, echoing Krause, Giner wrote in his *Estética*, 'Verdad, bondad y belleza son completamente conformes y hermanos entre sí, constituyendo como el acorde fundamental en la armonía y esencia de la vida' (p. 21). The artist, with this aesthetic vision, can set out the way forward to the regeneration of the nation's spiritual and moral health; he possesses 'la facultad de hacer algo efectivo, algo esencial en el tiempo'. Art is the stimulant to a new redemptive path. Unamuno, as ever, expressed this notion clearly in his *Amor y pedagogía* in 1903: 'el sentimiento [the intellectual's deepest yearnings] ... se refleja, mayor que en un sistema filosófico,

---

'Cartas de Antonio Machado a Juan Ramón Jiménez'; 'Relaciones amistosas ...'; 'Prosa y verso de Machado a Jiménez'; 'Prosa y verso de Jiménez a Machado', *La Torre*, VII, 25 (1959), 159–224.

en un poema en prosa o en verso, en una novela o leyenda' (II, 431). Thus the poet's sense of fallen ideals as expressed in a work was to form a mirror to the nation's own loss of confidence. The art of the *Helios* group and those, like Unamuno who supported them, and Machado's own poetry, was to hold up a mirror to this national sense of collapsing ideals by exploring their own dilemma and discovering through that art a possible way forward, to find hope amid their doubts and personal anguish, hope for self and hope for the *pueblo*.

For the new generation, then, there existed a close link between individual concerns and national spiritual and moral concerns. Their literary endeavour, arguably, is conditioned not only by purely aesthetic criteria but foremost by an art closely related to an idealistic ethical ideology. As Ernesto Bark, a radical member of the *Germinal* magazine group, noted at the height of this new fervour in *La santa bohemia* in 1913: 'nuestro ideal es *el arte vida* ... Las ideas-fuerzas se imponen irresistiblemente filtrándose en la conciencia en efluvios imperceptibles del arte y paulatinamente todo sentir y pensar de una nación'.[38] In this optimistic statement he expressed the collective view of his generation. Machado, for example, had just the year before published the first version of *Campos de Castilla*. It formed a part of the same campaign as he expressed in a letter to Jiménez in 1912 (*PrC*, III, 1518–19). Jiménez had published *Pastorales* in 1911 (written between 1905 and 1908) with a similar moral and spiritual artistic programme (Cardwell 2000b, 2007). Their art was shaped by an undefined idealism and by the longing for new vital directions with the aim of challenging the present crisis of moral and social decay, as Azorín noted in the Prologue to his *La fuerza del amor*: 'Hay entre nosotros, en la generación actual que empieza a vivir literariamente, una gran aspiración hacia el infinito, una ansia indeterminada a la idealidad. Desde este punto de vista, los escritores jóvenes de ahora ... son superiores ..., no por ser más artistas ni más exquisitos, sino porque su alma está más abierta a las ideas ambientes' (I, 737).

---

[38] Ernesto Bark, *La santa bohemia* (Madrid: Biblioteca Germinal, Editorial Coop. H. de Autores, 1913), p. 71.

A crisis of ideals and beliefs

At the same time they suffered personal crises of ideals and beliefs. In virtually all the new writers, including Machado, there is a shared sense of life's lost finality, a spiritual malaise which shaped their perception of the world about them (especially their homeland) and the direction their art was to take. Thus Gregorio Martínez Sierra in *Alma Española* on 6 March 1904, among many like voices: 'Dícese, y con razón, que la juventud actual, si no es frívola, es triste; yo creo que su frivolidad o tristeza son sencillamente desconcierto (mistrust), por falta de finalidad ... Antiguamente hablaba la Iglesia y daba la fórmula de vivir ...; hoy todo es silencio.' Thus the artist did not seek to recreate in Art a facsimile of reality (the now discredited school of Realism of the previous century, though much remained of its influence), nor offer concrete solutions for reform; rather, they sought to evoke something of the yearnings of the spirit, an approach pioneered by the much-admired Bécquer in the 1860s and continued in the work of Ricardo Gil and Francisco A. de Icaza (Cardwell 1972 and 1984b). As Jiménez put it in 1908 in a letter to Machado, 'Soñad siempre hacia el espíritu, nunca hacia la realidad' (*Libros de prosa*, 281). But the young writers filled with the hope of a better future for their fellow men felt oppressed by the feeling that any effort was ultimately pointless, as Machado admitted in poem LXXVII in the most laconic tone: 'la causa de esta angustia no consigo / ni vagamente comprender siquiera'. *Angustia* had been his companion since childhood: 'yo te conozco, / tú eres nostalgia de la vida buena / y soledad de corazón sombrío, / de barco sin naufragio y sin estrella'. He confesses to a mind caught between hope and despair like a storm-tossed ship without a compass bearing. Their pessimism at the lack of moral fibre and low intellectual horizons in Spain is matched by the belief in a directing élite which might bring progress through art with a stress on intense idealism. As Unamuno put it in 1905, 'Quisiéramos que el mundo fuera, no como es, sino como a nosotros se nos antoja (desperately desire) que debiera ser' (1905: I, 1268), a comment which speaks for the whole group. Yet disillusionment and a sense of hopelessness initiate in these young men not only a questioning of life's ultimate finality, the long-term effect of the negative Romantic response (Shaw 1972), but also a search for satisfying answers. Through literary endeavour, they believed, new values might be found, values they might offer the nation.

But the ideals to which they aspired are frustrated or crushed by reality. It is not the bustle of life, especially in cities where, by 1900, most of the nation lived, that they find their ideals, but in solitude, in books, in their imagination and in reverie, that is, in what Machado calls his 'galerías del alma', inner thoughts stimulated by memory, 'el don preclaro de evocar los sueños' (LXXXIX), and need. Terms like 'solo', 'soledad', 'ensueño', 'sueño', 'nostalgia', 'añoranza', 'recuerdo', 'memoria', 'fondo', 'dentro', 'rincón', 'refugio', 'corazón', images of interior worlds – caverns, crypts, passageways, galleries, endless 'caminos' – and, above all, 'alma' and 'espíritu' (all in *SGOP*) – are indicators of the trend of the artists' thoughts, and especially Machado's. They prefer inaction and the passivity of a nostalgic contemplation of past happiness or, as in the case of Machado's 'buen burgués' (XCI), or Azorín's man in a window in his *Castilla*, much admired by Machado who dedicted a poem to the book in *Campos* (CXVII), the nostalgic search for an impossible ideal.

Paradoxically, they also seek inspiration in travel. The study of landscape was an integral part of the curriculum in the Institición Libre and *excursionismo* became a popular activity among its pupils, including the Machados, and those associated with the Institución (Vila-Belda 2004 and 2006). As Ramsden notes, 'And in these excursions the young men sought the collective spirit of different periods and regions, for the collective, time-resistant spirit of the Spanish people through their history and into the present. But they also looked for themselves' (1974a, 207). The new generation evoke, like Machado himself, landscapes, vistas, gardens, plazas, that are 'tristes', 'soñolientos', in an atmosphere of 'dulce melancolía', a scene now 'gris' now 'triste'. The visible world, be it childhood Seville, the Guadarrama or the landscapes of Soria, becomes a screen onto which personal obsessions are projected, the classic Romantic and Symbolist pathetic fallacy, the *paisaje del alma / paisage d'âme* (Ribbans 2006). In their appeal to mental energy and human ideals, undermined by doubt, rather than to concrete reform, we find a conflict between idealistic action and a sense of defeat. And these conflicts are expressed, especially in the core of the *Helios* group –Machado, Jiménez, Martínez Sierra and Azorín – through melancholy landscapes, ruins, decaying gardens and broken humanity: old men (as in poems LXXXI and XCVI), the insane (CVI in *Campos*), humble seamstresses (XXXVIII), the sick, children, orphans, etc., all, like them, imagined victims (Cardwell 1981). As Ramsden has argued of Azorín, 'perhaps, amidst the general emptiness of life he even finds a curious satisfaction in communion with his grief' (Ramsden 1966, 170), a type of artistic masochism arguably expressed in the figure of Machado's contemplative 'buen burgués' (XCI). It gives strength to their art as, again, Azorín observed: 'El dolor es bello; él da al hombre el más intenso estado de conciencia; él hace meditar; él nos saca de la perdurable frivolidad humana' (1902: I, 890). It was a common sentiment.[39] Thus silence and solitude and the contemplation of broken humanity and decaying landscapes and ruins became a source of attraction. And solitude is less oppressive when the artist can evoke the past, the idyll of childhood or the spectacle of ruins or decay in the present. Thus, for Machado, memories of the Sevillian patio (poem VII) with its fountain and a shadow on the wall (a hint of a past – and lost – romantic love?), or of his mother and her pots of herbs, help him to come to terms with his sense of loss and – impossibly, despite his pessimism – he seeks to recover those memories. In some way the past seems preferable to the present; the past a repository for values and ideals the writer has lost. And the ravages of time are everywhere apparent in ancient churches and convents, in decaying mansions, in deserted plazas, abandoned gardens and avenues, in towering funeral cypress trees.[40] They also seek evidence of a time-

---

[39] See also Unamuno, a decade later, in *Del sentimiento trágico de la vida*, describing the positive effect of spiritual anguish: 'este nobilísimo, y el más profundo, y el más humano, y el más fecundo estado de alma, el de la desesperación ... Y han hecho del arte una religión y un remedio para el mal metafísico' (*O.C.*, 1911, XVI, 178–9). Such an attitude may have come from the widespread reading of Nietzsche who wrote in *The Gay Science*: 'Only great pain ... compels us to descend to ultimate depths ... I know it makes us more profound ... In the end, ... from such abysses, from such severe sickness, one returns newborn ... with merrier senses, with ... joy, more childlike and yet a hundred times subtler', ed. Walter Kaufmann (New York: Vintage, 1974), pp. 181–2. For Nietzsche's impact on finisecular writers see Gonzalo Sobejano, *Nietzsche en España* (Madrid: Gredos, 1967).

[40] Compare Pío Baroja's comment in 1926: 'En las ciudades los hombres de esta generación [the *gente nueva*] no buscarán las plazas elegantes, de aire parisiense o madrileño, preferirán visitar los barrios antiguos, los arrabales, y estarán siempre ansiosos de encontrar lo típico y lo característico', *Obras Completas* (Madrid: Biblioteca Nueva, 1946–51), V, p. 575.

resistant spirit of Spain in their quest for permanence. 'Comforted by an awareness of time's passing the writer seeks an escape from his obsessions and a fuller awareness of it. He seeks defences against it in the resistance to change of old towns, in the contemplation of nature and, finally, the permanence and immensity of the Spanish landscape' (Ramsden 1974b, 180). This is an obsessive theme in *SGOP*. The young writers like Machado and his circle seem to evoke the dying energies of Spain and, at the same time, a lost sense of timeless permanence. Machado seeks to evoke this mood and outlook in poems II, VIII, LXVI, XCVI and others as he hears the songs and cries of children in the street (III), a mysterious figure in a window (XV), girls sewing on a balcony (XXXVIII) or depicts a beggar in a decaying porch of a church (XXVI). But there is no discussion of the 'problem of Spain', nor any remedy suggested other than the appeal to a literary 'war' to regenerate the nation. Spain, past and present, becomes expressions of personal concerns, especially later for Machado in *Campos de Castilla*. Decaying churches and convents (X, XXXI) are also an expression of a loss of faith, for which faith the writer hankers with nostalgia. It is possible, in his first visit to Paris, that he had read *Bruges la Morte* (1892) of Georges Rodenbach, a book which spawned a whole series of imitations and glosses (Lozano 1990). There remains, in spite of the abandonment of some of the more effusive poems of *S*, many hints of the Decadence in *SGOP*: the closed garden of suffering, crumbling monuments and decaying towns, gathering darkness, solitary paths, references to Greek myth, even menacing *femmes fatales* complete with *fleurs du mal* (XVI, XXX).

What unites Machado and the *Helios* group are their remarkable remembered realities. They are often coloured by *ensueño* and, too, evoked in a dreamlike halo or by the rays of the setting sun: consider poems XIII and XVII. The process, in turn, suggests beauty, stillness and, above all, permanence. Against the sense of collapsed ideals and the destructive forces of time and death, their observation and interpretation of reality offered a comfort. It was not the reality before them but their inner spirit of things, what Machado calls the 'misterio', which they sought to evoke. But the search for that 'misterio' for Machado was fraught with danger as he admitted to Unamuno in a letter in May 1904: 'La belleza no está en el misterio, sino en el deseo de penetrarlo. Pero este camino es muy peligroso y puede llevarnos a hacer el caos en nosotros mismos si no caemos en la vanidad de crear sistemáticamente brumas que, en realidad, no existen, no deben existir' (*PrC*, III, 1474). In a series of poems – XXXVII, LXIII, for example – evoking a symbolic journey inwards in search of meaning, Machado depicts, as the letter suggests, a tableau of mental chaos set against the desire for a guiding nucleus.

He suffered from the same spiritual problems as those of his generation and, in many ways, followed similar paths, paths they took in their attempts to restore a positive consensus of intellectual thought in Spain and their endeavours to reconstruct the nation's – and their own – sense of vital purpose and existential belief. As we shall see in what follows, Machado belonged intellectually in his aspirations and his writing to the patterns of concerns outlined above. Thus we might refute again the claim that he moved in a separate sphere from his contemporaries.

The search for meaning

Many critics have pointed to the poet's obsession with time and passing time and the emptiness of the present. He see-saws between 'esperanzas y recuerdos' (CXXII) and 'todo lo que ya se fue' (XCIII). And this spiritual unease pervades his poems. In probing the past through memory, reverie and his innermost thoughts, his 'galerías del alma', he finds moments of hope always tainted by a sense of loss. Decaying gardens and flowers, fountains and rivers, fading light and distant inaccessible horizons, closed glass spaces suggesting *serres chaudes* (heated conservatories, a major Symbolist motif), all the heritage of the Symbolist Decadence and his years in Paris, suggest impossible illusions and failing ideals. Poem VI is a case in point where longing (in the return to a garden visited in the past and associated with 'un sueño lejano' and 'antiguos delirios de amores') is contrasted with reality where past and present collide. In effect, Machado recreates the negative Romantic juxtaposition of illusion and reality most pithily expressed in José de Espronceda's *Canto a Teresa* from his *El diablo mundo* (1840): 'el bien pasado, el dolor presente'. While the 'tarde' is 'clara' it becomes the bearer of the poet's obsessions. Yet the 'tarde' cannot be 'triste y soñolienta'; it is the poet who is sad, who dreams. As with his contemporaries, he employs the Romantic and Symbolist trope of the pathetic fallacy and the *paysage d'âme* where reality takes on the contours and emotions of the writer. As Azorín noted in his review of *Campos de Castilla* in 1913, 'la característica de Machado, la que marca y define su obra es la objetivación del poeta en el paisaje que describe ... Paisaje y sentimientos – modalidad psicológica – son una misma cosa; el poeta se traslada al objeto descrito y en la manera de describirlo nos da su propio espíritu', II, p. 809. The poet inserts himself into the landscape and it becomes subjective in the poet. *SGOP* has many such examples. Passing time is evoked in the overgrown ivy, thick with dust in poem V (see also poem XCI). The grating of the key and the 'agrio ruido' as the *cancela* opens suggests rust and, thus too, time's erosion. Alone, the fountain (a typical popular image in traditional verse, here recreated as a *copla*) becomes the interlocutor in this internal dialogue/monologue. It stimulates apparently timeless memories – 'lo mismo que ahora' – which the poet seeks to recall in vain. And so, aware that past bitterness seems far off – 'que es lejana la amargura mía' – he seeks 'mi alegre leyenda olvidada'. But that experience is merely a 'leyenda' not a reality, even if one in the past. Thus, more powerfully than Espronceda's contrast of a lost past felicity and a present despair, Machado intensifies and alters the contrast in the revelation in this internalised interrogation that 'Yo no sé leyenda de antigua alegría, / sino historias viejas de melancolía'. These verses recapitulate the sense of poem LXXVI. There was no past happiness nor love to be recovered in this symbolic journey into memory. The poet came 'solo con tu pena'; his anxious search unquenched, 'la sed que ahora tienen [tus labios], entonces tenían'. And the poem closes as it began as the symbolic gate of memory closes in this powerful and emotional poem, an extraordinary reprise of Verlaine's 'Après trois ans' from *Fêtes galantes* (1869) which Machado knew from his Paris days (Ribbans 1957a, b, 1968/69, 1976/77, 1979; Ilie 1962; Ferreres 1975).

This sense of loss permeates *SGOP*, mostly expressed in an indirect, often unstated form. In poem LXVIII the scent of jasmine on the breeze (evocation of an Andalusian patio) again recalls memories. While the poet seeks the perfume of roses (again an indirect mono-dialogue) suggesting lost happiness, the unidentified interlocutor reveals that there are no fresh flowers to be had. The poet will leave with the 'llanto' of fountains (in reality his own distress) and the autumnal, thus decaying, dying effects of yellowing leaves and faded petals. Based, again, on a *copla* Machado creates anew an internal debate, seeking happiness for his 'corazón' yet confronted with decay and death. The traditional *copla* of flowers, gardens and love is transformed into a simple internal mono-dialogue in Symbolist terms of suggestion and nuance. In poem LV, specifically entitled 'Hastío', the relentless weight of time symbolised in the insistent tick of the clock – 'el tictac acompasado / odiosamente golpea' – is experienced by the poet; it is he, not the clock who feels the 'odio'. This image is underlined by the plashing of the fountain and the darkening day (both time markers). The pain felt in the final line ends in an ellipsis (the verbal equivalent of a sigh) and is completed in the image of withered foliage which 'weeps'. Again Machado overlays emotions on inanimate objects; it is the poet who weeps, not the 'fronda marchita'. More in tune with the less nuanced expression of sadness of other Andalusian poets like Reina, Durbán Orozco, Reyes or Villaespesa, yet muted by the Symbolist figuring of 'penas' as natural elements, the poet admits what, more indirectly, he had learned in poem VI: that he had never enjoyed happiness in the past. The negative Romantic contrast of past and present is transmuted into the more negative contrast of 'ayer dolores' and 'hoy mariposas negras', this latter again a popular image at the end of the nineteenth century. Yet past anguish was nevertheless fruitful –silk worms, flowers, bees; now his pain is evoked in choking weeds, charred corn, woodworms. What is crucial here is not that the poet has lost a former happiness; rather, that his earlier 'dolores' were fruitful, they produced symbolic and positive outcomes: silk, wax, honey. His 'dolores / tenían lágrimas buenas' associated with the well and an irrigated orchard, all elements again taken from popular song. Machado expresses a poetic version of Azorín's 'el dolor es bello' with the rider that, later, his present 'dolor' will be less productive in the *guerra literaria* to engender national spiritual aspirations. It is an example of the mood swings of the collection as a whole. Evoking the image of the beehive for a time in the past (a motif repeated in other poems of *SGOP* and taken from Greek myth and mystic writings) he now faces a wall which blocks his way back and forwards. In poem XCV, 'Coplas mundanas' (written in the *redondilla* form of the *copla*), Machado again contrasts past and present, lamenting the passing of his youth, presumably his bohemian past in Paris and Madrid at the turn of the century. He was about 31 at the time of this poem's composition, and still without a permanent occupation. Again, he contrasts the past, the 'galerías del recuerdo' a typical Symbolist trope of internal frames and spaces (see Cardwell 1985a, 1987, 1989b, 1990, 1997a; Meyers 1954; Ruiz Ramón 1962a; Zardoya 1961), with a darker present. He bids adieu to an earlier fruitful phase, expressed in terms of the fountain, 'aguas sonoras' and fertilising rain, to face a world where gold is transmuted into base copper. As Azorín had noted, spiritual anguish heightens awareness, provokes thought, makes the sufferer stand outside 'la perdurable frivolidad humana'.

How did this generational process of thought come about? We must return to the growing belief, fuelled by an all-pervasive Krausism and the influence of the Institución Libre, that the artist was, as Shelley had set out in his *Defence of Poetry* (1821), a legislator for the future and a secular redeemer in the new *guerra literaria*.[41] Shelley's message, combined with Spain's intellectual interpretation of Krause's secular messianism was totally absorbed by the end of the century. Darío, in *Los raros* (1896), as noted above, spoke of 'el sacerdocio (priesthood) o misión de la belleza'. But Ganivet, in 1898, also spoke of 'una hermandad de trabajadores espirituales', Unamuno in 1902 of 'redentores'(redeemers) and 'intelectuales'; Alejandro Sawa (the blind poet of Valle-Inclán's *Luces de bohemia*) wrote in 1905 of the poet as 'un sembrador (sower) de ideas ... trabajadores de la idea'; Jiménez later creates an 'ética-estética' and Ortega spoke of 'los mejores', a new directing intellectual élite (Cardwell 1985b and 2013; Gullón 1959).

---

[41] A translation of the *Defence* was available in Spain as *Defensa de la poesía y otros ensayos* (Madrid: Leonard Williams) in 1904. Jiménez owned a copy which he heavily annotated. See Howard T. Young, *The Line in the Margin: Juan Ramón Jiménez and his Readings in Blake, Shelley and Yeats* (Madison: University of Wisconsin Press, 1980).

La guerra literaria

Azorín, in his own *Soledades* of 1898, set out the necessary ethics of the modern artist. The echoes of the Institución and Giner de los Ríos are clear: 'No basta con ser sabios; es preciso ser buenos. El artista que piensa noblemente y no vive como piensa, no es un artista completo. No hay vida pública ni vida privada, no hay más que una idea honesta' (1898: I, 181). Six years later, now a friend of Machado, Azorín had refined his message in his journal *Alma Española* (3-I-1904). 'Este arte inutilitario e incorruptible', he wrote,

> [T]iene una utilidad única, excepcional, maravillosa, suprema: porque él hace que nos sintamos todos los hombres unos, solidarios, amorosos, ante estas sensaciones extraordinarias de belleza, que sólo nosotros sobre la tierra somos capaces de sentir y gozar; y porque él, que es producto de la fina sensibilidad de unos pocos, ha afinado la sensibilidad de las masas y ha preparado así una nueva conciencia social.

Note the stress on the role of the artist and art in the process of the redemption and regeneration of the masses through the revelation of his own dilemmas and the appeal to personal behaviour and morality, always invested with the discourses of religion, to give authority to their faith.[42] How could art and self-help effect such an enterprise? An article by Gregorio Martínez Sierra in Azorín's *Alma Española* in the same 1904 issue and on the same page as Azorín's assertion offers a further clue. Speaking of the sadness of his fellow artists he insists that 'de esta tristeza que es sentimiento deprimente y enervador [los jóvenes] saben sacar aliento para el trabajo y hacen su labor incansable'. He continued:

> ¿Labor inútil? ¿Actividad estéril? Bondadosamente hay quienes les amonesta ¡Trabajad por la vida! Yo sé que para ellos la vida es la belleza, y que son sus versos y sus prosas la única razón de su vivir. Y sé también que no es su esfuerzo inútil; en todo pueblo son los ideales de belleza sustentados por unos pocos, el granito (tiny grain) de sal que asegura la persistencia de la civilización.

---

[42] Once more we note the voice of Shelley and that of the Krausists of the Institución who, like Shelley, subsumed aesthetics and ethics as a single entity in the preparation of the ideal man, a combination expressed succinctly by Jiménez with his 'ética-estética.' The idea goes back to the Krausists of the mid-century before.

He was not alone in pointing to sadness as a potent force for regeneration as the reviews of Manuel Machado's *Alma* and the verses of José Asunción Silva by Unamuno demonstrate. To 'sadness' as a motor force I shall return. So: idealism, the creation of a select group of talent, almost religious in its fervour and which, through its special sensitivity and their specific melancholic view of life can offer specific insights, such men might offer a programme for the spiritual redemption and regeneration of the nation. This, I submit, was a generational aspiration and has nothing, absolutely nothing, to do with any supposed *enfrentamiento* of two opposed groups: *modernismo v noventayocho*.

Let us look at Machado again. In the Prologue to his *Páginas escogidas* of 1917, with obvious echoes of Giner and Unamuno, he wrote of his faith in terms of

> una honda palpitación del espíritu; lo que pone el alma, ... si es que algo dice, con voz propia, en respuesta animada al contacto del mundo. Y aún pensaba que el hombre puede sorprender algunas palabras de un íntimo monólogo, distinguiendo la voz viva de los ecos inertes [passive echoes]; que puede también, mirando hacia dentro, vislumbrar [glimpse] los ideales cordiales, los universales del sentimiento.

To understand these sentiments we need to go back to his return from Paris in 1899 and, more pertinently, his second return in early 1903, when he began the correspondence with Unamuno and Jiménez and friendship with the latter. The poet had asked him to review his recently published *Arias tristes*, Jiménez's fourth collection. Machado stresses the importance of the book as a message to those less sensitive than Jiménez and his group, even ignorant, and thus, by implication in the messianic view of the time, in want of moral or spiritual reform. He wrote, 'Estoy dispuesto a que esa obra se critique y a enterar [sic] a las gentes de muchas cosas que no saben' (*PrC*, III, 1458). That is, poets must teach the masses who are sunk in an inauthentic life, in order to bring them to the 'light' and the 'conciencia' of the new ideal. This echoes Jiménez's review of Timoteo Orbe's *Rejas de oro* of 1900 and of Rafael Leyda's *Valle de lágrimas* in 1903 in *Helios*, where Jiménez insists 'Hoy, más que nunca, tenemos una juventud que quiere trabajar, y que trabaja, y que va adelante, y que empieza a imponerse en todas partes' (*Libros de prosa*, 250). Machado replies that he would happily write for *Helios*, '¿y por qué no? ¿Acaso no es allí donde elaboramos el arte de mañana? ¿No es la única revista que mantiene la juventud y el amor a la belleza?' (*PrC*, III, 1458). Azorín in *Alma Española* in 1904, noted that 'el arte es el principal factor de la revolución' and exhorted his friends to 'Contribuid con vuestro arte a la creación de una patria nueva' just as for Machado, also in 1904, who wrote 'es necesario que antes triunfe la estética' (*PrC*, III, 1473). But what do the inauthentic masses lack and art provide? Machado continues in the same letter to Jiménez: 'He de hacer algo sincero, lleno de verdad y de amor, no un bombo ridículo [a stupid drum dance] ni una crítica de ratón [critical fluff]' and ends by praising the 'admirable' and the 'alma' of his friend's verses and affirming the belief shared in rejecting the 'éxito ... la pedantería ... la vanidad ...' It is necessary, he went on, to wage a great struggle against an ignoble rabble nourished in a vile world. 'Pero hay que luchar sabiendo que los fuertes somos nosotros ... yo protesto ... ¿Y V?...., V protesta como yo'. Clearly this is an expression of intense faith shared in common. At the same time Machado saw himself at a crossroads, after the publication of *S* early the year before, as he noted to Jiménez: 'No estoy muy satisfecho de las cosas que hago últimamente. Estoy en un período de evolución y todavía no he encontrado la forma de expresión de mi nueva poesía'. Hence the experiments at various prosodic forms, mainly popular forms, in *SGOP* listed in the Notes to the Poems. But how does Machado's poetry at this time express this 'protest', especially in the period when these militant terms had clear revolutionary and political overtones? A study of the review itself offers clues. He stresses, as had Unamuno, the 'sentimiento deprimente' of his generation in the struggle to foment new attitudes. He also stresses the role that this select minority might offer to 'trabajar por la vida y despertar conciencias'; that is, identify the hidden 'alma' and create a new generation of ideal men through a heightened culture and a special vision. Through this process, it was confidently assumed, the nation could be regenerated as Unamuno confidently predicted in 'Nicodemo el fariseo' in 1901. The duty of the intellectuals, Unamuno wrote, is to reject the politics of the ruling classes; rather to study the *pueblo* to discover 'las raíces de su espíritu' (IV, 1047). Of this 'espíritu' Machado is to speak in the prologues to his later works, in the review of Unamuno's *Contra esto y aquello* in 1905 and in the Mairena musings. Thus, Machado can approve, in his review of *Arias tristes*, of Jiménez's 'sensibilidad fina y vibrante, acaso llega a lastimar al alma, antes de despertarla' (*PrC*, III, 1469). Mark and wound the soul of the reader and he will surely awaken to an appropriate vision for the nation and his fellows. Notice the hidden religious discourse of illumination and/or martyrdom here, very much the language of the time and linked with a prevalent *neomisticismo* which will be explored below. Jiménez's poems produce, Machado suggests, 'una trepidación [pulse] más honda ... que llega a embriagar [enrapture] el alma'; they represent 'una nebulosa esperanza de algo que ha de vivirse un día' (*PrC*, III, 1469). We find echoes of Jiménez's own statements at this time and, as we have seen, his and Machado's contemporaries. If anything, we witness a consistent finisecular theme. Are not these statements of Machado's and his fellow writers a counter to the *enfrentamiento* argument and its description of *modernismo* as an art of escape, ivory-towered, artificial and decadent? Machado might accuse Jiménez of being overly introspective when he enquires '¿no seríamos capaces de soñar con los ojos abiertos en la vida activa, en la vida militante?' (*PrC*, III, 1470) (note the language of 'war') a statement which suggests that he, too, found difficulty in balancing his exploration of the 'galerías del alma' in search of an authentic self with the search for some form of nucleus or idea for the nation which he defines, in an echo of Unamuno, as 'los ideales cordiales ... universales' or the 'fondo eterno', an ideal which Unamuno had already mentioned in a letter to Machado. This question of the sincerity of the poet's task and the dangers inherent in a struggle which might be self-deceiving rather than one of a discovery of something beyond, some vital absolute, was to be for his mentor Unamuno, as for himself, an obsessive theme. The problem rests, as Machado insists in this review, that 'una poesía que aspire a conmover a todos, ha de ser muy íntimo. ... Pero mientras nuestra alma no se despierte para elevarse, será en vano que ahondemos [search inwards] en nosotros mismos' (*PrC*, III, 1470). That is, he does not seek after fancies or artificial effects (hence the rejection of certain poems from the first *Soledades*) but rather to discover his intimate 'self' which, in turn, would reveal the hidden depths of humanity itself. That, in turn, would reveal the nucleus and base for a personal and collective regeneration. Machado returned to this theme in a review of Unamuno's *Vida de don Quijote y Sancho* in 1905:

> Sus bellos sermones... son ... palabras vivificadoras ... que exhortan a una interna renovación. Y fuerza es confesar que algo, aunque poco, se adelanta. Existe hoy más trajín espiritual, ... de enseñar, de trabajar, que en la época anterior ... Vamos en busca de mejor vida. Los gestos de protesta, de rebeldía, de iconoclasticismo, de injusticia si queréis, ... ¿qué son en el fondo, sino ese noble deseo de renovación? (*PrC*, III, 1480)

In the context of the value the young generation placed on its own melancholia and its metaphysical doubts Machado attempts to define the possible power of his 'inquietudes y profundas y eternas torturas'. This is the basis for the 'protest' of the generation. His own doubts and melancholy would furnish the motor force for change alongside other forces for reform:

> Y los gestos de compunción [regret], de tristeza, de melancolía, y las palabras plañideras y elegíacas [plaintive, elegiac] de la juventud más lírica, ¿qué son sino expresión del mismo desconcierto [mistrust] y ansia de nueva vida? Las diferencias son sólo de procedimiento [procedure, method]. (*PrC*, III, 1481)

One might cavil at this assertion and those of Machado's contemporaries, but it was, I submit, a notion held widely and forcibly among the young writers of the *Helios* group and its wider circles. We find a reformulation of this idea by Machado as late as 1936 amid another 'disaster' for the Spanish nation. Unamuno appears again in Machado's argument, especially the idea of the 'vidente' elaborated nearly forty years before in *En torno al casticismo* and Unamuno's reviews of Manuel Machado's *Alma* and the verses of Silva. Machado wrote in 1936, 'Pensaba mi maestro [Unamuno] que la poesía, aun la más amarga, era siempre un acto vidente, de afirmación de una realidad absoluta' (*PrC*, IV, 2045). This is a theme Machado had touched on in the review of *La vida de don Quijote y Sancho* in 1905,

> Toda labor individual tiende – en el arte, al menos – a hacerse más intensa, cada cual se busca a sí mismo, y pretende labrar su propio terrón [patch] espiritual ... Ya por labor introspectiva se marcha poco a poco a conocer la psicología de este pueblo [equals *alma nacional*], tan profundamente ignorante de sí mismo. (*PrC*, III, 1471)

In this statement Machado summarises all the points made above. The melancholic artist, victim of his own metaphysical doubts, is a redeemer who can save the nation given the abject spiritual condition in which it finds itself: a widespread idea by 1905. In the review of *Arias tristes* two years earlier he had insisted on the presence of the idealistic potential and the spiritual disquiet of modern poetry as the necessary engine for change (*PrC*, III, 1471).

Later, in 1913, on sending Jiménez a copy of a poem he had dedicated to Azorín's *Castilla* he added a note:

> Intento en ella de colocarme en el punto inicial de unas cuantas almas selectas y continuar en mí mismo esos varios impulsos ... hacia una mira ideal y lejana. Si no formamos una sola corriente vital e impetuosa, la inercia española triunfará. (*PrC*, III, 1518)

How did this 'mira ideal y lejana' (note that 'trace' revealing that the process would be a long-term one) express itself? A common theme is the legacy of the negative Romantic response, the insistent expression of doubt and scepticism. One of the major aspects of the early work, shared with his contemporaries, is how can man overcome the awareness of time leading to inevitable death with no redemption? How can one face with serenity, even equanimity, the sense of an oppressive present? Listen to Machado in his early verses: '¿Adónde el camino irá?' (XI); 'Yo meditaba absorto, devanando / los hilos del hastío y la tristeza' (XIV). These are sentiments we immediately associate with Ganivet, Unamuno, Baroja, Azorín, Villaespesa, Juan Ramón and others. One pattern of escape is through Art. Art, they believed was a spiritual and religious force so that, through it, the artist could seek some form of spiritual rebirth or a world where time and insight have no sway. Such a belief lies at the core of the Krausist ethic as we have seen, but such a pattern might also explain the popularity for the Symbolist-Decadence filtered through essays on and translations of Baudelaire and Gautier's 'Notice' to *Les Fleurs du mal*, the poetry of Verlaine and Samain and Bourget's *Essai de psycologie contemporaine* (1885), all available in the review press. Pedro González Blanco, member of the *Helios* Brotherhood, writing of Samain in *Helios* itself in 1903, noted: '[E]n poesía, para ser sencillo, no hay más que seguir el consejo de Verlaine, esto es, llegar a la plena posesión de sí mismo'. To be oneself or discover oneself in the terms set out by Samain, Verlaine and Baudelaire in his *Le peintre de la vie moderne*, especially the sections on the *dandy*, and the essay 'La modernité', was to be the modern artist. This latter essay, arguably, gave its name to the new movement, *modernismo*, not the *modernismo* of recent critical discourses or polar opposite of a so-called *noventayocho*, but in its original meaning, a sense of the modern which offered the promise of a spiritual regeneration for the artist and, thus, regeneration for the reader. Besides, as Azorín had argued as early as 1895, art and the cult of artifice (*modernismo* as the Decadence) was the mark of the true artist:

> La poesía moderna ... es lo extraordinario, lo artificial, si se quiere. El verdadero poeta hace algo más que copiar: crea, corrige. Corrige la naturaleza, y al corregirla estampa en ella su sello original, inimitable. Copiar de copias ajenas [other people's] es labor de máquinas; hacer lo que nadie ha hecho, lo que se desvía [swerves away] de la tradición, es labor de artista. (I, 183)

It is a sentiment Darío would repeat a year later in the *Palabras liminares* to *Prosas profanas* in 1896. If there are echoes of Baudelaire in Azorín's claim, there is also an echo of the essays on Oscar Wilde by Enrique Gómez Carrillo in *Sensaciones de arte* of 1891. It was this same critic, in the essay 'El neomisticismo' in *Literatura extranjera* (Paris: Garnier) of 1895 (p. 300), who caught the new spirit which was to take form in 1902. In a direct echo of Baudelaire's 'Enivrez vous', Gómez Carrillo characterised the new aesthetic as a type of 'borrachera'. Not merely alcoholic inebriation but a state of spiritual intoxication as a defence against the loss of faith and idealism. The older generation of Krausists like Urbano González Serrano, later intimate of the *Helios* group, polymath and critic, noted as early as 1881 the presence of:

> corrientes misteriosas e influencias poderosísimas, de virtualidad innegable, del arte a la religión y viceversa ... entendiendo que un *ideal estético* [his italics] puede guiar a un ideal religioso ... Así, al lado de la desesperación, hállase ... un rasgo de energía y virtualidad potentísima, una alta aspiración a algo, que por lo que tiene de vago e indeterminado encanta y seduce y constituye como el bálsamo [balm] de consuelo, que restaña [staunch] heridas aún abiertas.[43]

---

[43] Urbano González Serrano, *Ensayos de crítica y filosofía* (Madrid: Imp. Hernández, 1881), pp. 93–4. The language of healing here echoes similar statements by the early Romantics, especially Nicomedes Pastor-Díaz. See Cardwell, '"Un monarca de la bohemia": Alejandro Sawa, la *gente nueva* y el momento finisecular. Patologías y semblanzas', *Hispanic Journal*, 34, 2 (2013), 29–44.

It would appear that the young men of the *fin de siglo* sought to attain a state of being where they might transcend, even if temporarily, their scepticism and doubts. I suggest that the idea of Art and literary creation offered a new religion, a type of spiritual inebriation, the expression of deep emotions as a remedy for their ills and, through their work, outwards to their readers and society. Where Spain's backwardness – economically, politically, militarily, the failure of the Church – had led to suffering without any obvious remedy, and the crushing of hopes for the future, an art which converted aesthetic pleasure into *neomisticismo* or spiritual elevation and rebirth (with the works of Thomas à Kempis, Santa Teresa and San Juan de la Cruz in mind, works cited and reviewed in the press and debated in the Real Academia and the Ateneo), and the creation of a world immune to the trials of real life caught in time were potently attractive. While the artist might contemplate his *dolor* and *hastío*, his moments of aesthetic and neo-mystic transcendence would lead to the potential for 'regeneration', the buzzword of the age. In 1883, in *Cuestiones contemporáneas*, González Serrano identified 'una fe invertida' which countered the growing scepticism of the time.[44] A year later he returned to this theme in an essay entitled 'El dolor', again stressing the heterodox nature of this new phenomenon:

> Avanza la juventud e idealiza el amor hasta llegar al límite de lo místico... el movimiento lógico y expansivo del amor en la *Imitación de Cristo* ... [se convierte] en amores ... sedientos de ideal. Lo mismo se observa en los poetas. ... Sentir su propia miseria es elevarse por encima de ella.[45]

Personal suffering must lead to a love of one's fellow men, the very message of the *Helios* 'paladines' in the *guerra literaria*. In 1903, that *annus mirabilis* of the young generation, in an essay in *La literatura del día*, González Serrano returned to his theme. '*Modernismo*' (by which he meant the new literature), he noted,

> huye con honda melancolía de la fe perdida, y emprende su marcha hacia *terra incognita* con la esperanza moral del Nuevo Mesianismo, ... con sed insaciable del ideal y llega a ser místico secularizado y

---

[44] Urbano González Serrano, *Cuestiones contemporáneas* (Madrid: G. Hernández, 1883), p. 7.

[45] Urbano González Serrano, *En pro y en contra (Críticas)* (Madrid: Sucesores de Rivadeneyra, 1894), p. 98.

heterodoxo o *ateo por bondad*. Oscilan entre su escepticismo y un misticismo cerebral, escape de energías.[46]

Does this not describe exactly the writings of Azorín, Baroja, Unamuno, Jiménez and, especially, that of Antonio Machado at this time? Azorín, Machado's friend, in 1902 (Lozano 2006) for example, made the point that personal *dolor* would lead both to insight and spiritual refinement, raise one above the 'frivolity' of a decadent age, as we have noted: 'El dolor es bello' (I, 890). Much later, amid the aftermath of the Spanish Civil War, his exile and the attack on Pearl Harbor in 1941, Jiménez looked in his *El trabajo gustoso (Conferencias)* (Mexico: Aguilar, 1961), for an artistic 'aristócrata' who would:

> llegar a lo mejor, ayudar a integrar una sociedad mayor ... La tristeza serena es una forma superior de vida, como la serena alegría. Hay que buscar el equilibrio entre lo alegre y lo triste y encontrarlo a cada estremo su valor. De la fuente de la tristeza surten también aguas riquísimas de amor, de paz de dicha (pp. 80 and 49).

If politicians were to read poetry every day, he added, the world would be a better place: this no more than a reiteration of Machado's review of Unamuno's *Vida de don Quijote y Sancho* in 1905 and various pronouncements Machado made in Valencia towards the end of the Civil War. Faced with profound national crises these men, it would appear, fell back on the same idealism they had espoused in the early years of the new century. The appearance of the 'new', where personal distress offered itself as a secular spiritual elevation, one commented on by a whole host of critics and, most pertinently, in Machado's letters and articles, was, I submit, the manifest of the young writers' attempt to regenerate themselves and the nation as *videntes* and *redentores*. It was the opening up to other European (mainly English and French) cultures that stimulated what was genuinely 'modern', a recognition of something of value and significance which responded to the needs of the moment after the slow collapse of Spain's institutions from the Restoration onwards and the aftermath of the Disasters of 1898. It was a brave initiative, but more realistic and potent forces were at work which were to clash in July 1936 and to erase from the Franco

---

[46] Urbano González Serrano, 'El Satanismo y el modernismo en el arte', *La literatura del día (1890 a 1903)* (Barcelona: Imp. de Heinrich y Cía, 1903), pp. 33–4.

Academy and a new generation of readers this messianic message and convert it into an art which was typified in entirely negative terms (feminine, cosmopolitan, *parisino*, alienated, neurotic, sick) as against a more robust, healthy and masculine supposed Generation of 1898.

Antonio Machado, *neomisticismo* and Symbolism

The association of *fin de siglo* artistic idealism, scepticism and a waning religious belief is, then, a marked feature of the writing of Machado's circle and its wider links with the Krausists and the men of the Institución of the 1880s and 1890s. J. López Morillas, in his *Hacia el 98*, with reference to these men (Sanz del Río, Fernando de Castro, Giner, Azcárate, guides who all shaped Machado's outlook) spoke of a 'crisis de la conciencia española' (López Morillas 1972, 119–59). One response to this crisis was to elaborate a new secular religion, one based on Spanish tradition and on its unique literature of mystical revelation (see Ramsden 1974b, 155–72). The new generation were, as Ramsden has argued, 'religious spirits without faith, sceptics tormented by their scepticism, atheistic mystics' (Ramsden 1974a, 34). 'Se puede ser místico ateo', wrote Unamuno in 1892. A year later Ganivet confessed to 'un especie de misticismo negativo'. In 1902 Baroja referred to his hero Ossorio's state of mind as 'misticidad'. Azorín wrote of his *alter ego*'s 'misticismo ateo' in the same year. Machado refers to himself as 'un filósofo trasnochado' (XCV) and, in early 1913, he wrote to Jiménez to confess that 'Mi pensamiento está generalmente ocupado por lo que llama Kant conflictos de las ideas trascendentales y busco en la poesía un alivio a esta ingrata tarea. En el fondo soy un creyente en una realidad espiritual opuesta al mundo sensible' (*PrC*, III, 1524) (Baker 1985; Pérez Gago 1984). Clearly, the reaction to a sense of fallen values created the need for some form of unorthodox religious response even if it seemed insubstantial as Unamuno noted in a letter to Leopoldo Alas, critic of the 'new' literature, on 9 May 1900: '¡Ah!, qué triste es después de una niñez y juventud de fe sencilla haberla perdido en vida ultraterrena, y buscar en nombre, fama y Gloria un miserable remedo (parody) de ella.'[47]

---

[47] Miguel de Unamuno, *Epistolario a Clarín* (Madrid: Pueyo, 1951), pp. 33–103 (p. 84).

We have noted the assessments of Urbano González Serrano over nearly a decade which chronicle the rise of an unorthodox form of 'mystical' religion. 'El *Modernismo*', he noted in 1903, 'huye con honda melancolía de la fe perdida ... con sed insaciable del ideal y llega a ser místico secularizado y heterodoxo o *ateo por bondad*' (note 46). To express one's spiritual doubt and existential anguish and see it as a potential spiritual force, as Azorín was to note – 'el dolor es bello' – had become a commonplace. Machado, too, attests that writing might lead to 'una alta aspiración a algo' as a result of personal scepticism. The artist is, as Azorín puts it in his *Diario de un enfermo* of 1901, is 'un nostálgico de ideal' (I, 691).

Machado's own doubts become almost obsessional in his early verses. He looks for 'un algo que pasa / y nunca llega' (X), speaks of 'una alegre leyenda olvidada' (VI), asks '¿Adónde el camino irá?' (XI) and '¿Dónde están los huertos floridos...?' (XLIII) (employing the trope of a lost garden / paradise from popular poetry and tradition), and, cautiously, he probes: '¿Al fin la alegría se acerca?' (XLIII). Longing for an ideal or a finality is countered by constant doubts. Like his contemporaries he looks for a new belief which, as Ramsden (1974b) has convincingly argued, is to be discovered in a past of more certain faith, especially in literature (which is, in reality, a search for self) and in the creation for the artist of a new role as a saviour and priest. We have seen how Krause, through Sanz del Río's translation and its transmission through the Institución and its teachers, had expressed his new messianic message in terms of a secular religion; the artist's role a 'sacerdocio'[priesthood]. Taken up by writers as distinct as Darío, with his poet as 'un lamentable cristo del arte', and Unamuno's description of the writer as a 'redentor' (redeemer), the idea had become a commonplace. It is no coincidence that there was considerable intellectual interest in the mystical and religious writers of the medieval past: San Francisco, Tomas à Kempis, Santa Teresa, Fray Luis de León and San Juan de la Cruz, the latter the subject of a lecture by Marcelino Menéndez Pelayo, the polymath of the late century, and essays by Emilia Pardo Bazán, major novelist and critic. But they were read in a new fashion, as González Serrano had noted. Literary creation, it seems, was seen as a moral, even spiritual/religious duty. In May 1904 Machado wrote to Unamuno to declare that 'yo veo la poesía como un yunque [anvil] de constante actividad espiritual, no como un taller [workshop] de fórmulas dogmáticas revestidas [dressed up] de imágenes más o menos brillantes' (*PrC*, III, 1473) a theme he took up later in 1912 in *Los complementarios* (*PrC,* III, 1208–12). Writing was more than creating lyrical effects; it was a spiritual quest and a moral duty. It seems that Machado was at a turning point in 1904, an augury of the changes he would make in the final *SGOP*. That change in outlook has a specific aim: to offer a spiritual message to his fellows. 'Todos nuestros esfuerzos deben tender hacia la luz, hacia la conciencia. He aquí el pensamiento que debía unirnos a todos,' he wrote in the same letter (*PrC*, III, 1473). He acknowledged that Unamuno had been a model who had encouraged the new writers to break with the old, a mentor who had made him reject his earlier ideals and, in part, poetic practice.[48] He continued:

> Y hoy digo: es verdad, hay que soñar despierto. No debemos crearnos un mundo aparte en que gozar fantástica y egoísticamente de la contemplación de nosotros mismos; no debemos huir de la vida para forjarnos una vida mejor que sea estéril para los demás. (1474)

He recognised that his verses must reach out to the nation, form part of the new *guerra literaria.* Yet, while he might long for some form of secularised faith, the revealing paradoxical phrase 'bendita ilusión' (LIX) reveals considerable doubts. It was the Symbolist aesthetic with its emphasis on 'absences' and 'pure' notions, its use of mirrors, glass, windows, enclosed gardens and, especially, its imagery of spaces which folded ever inwards to a vanishing point and paths which led to distant impossible horizons, often illuminated by setting suns and fading light, which proved the means to set out a new poetic credo.

It may have been a reading of Mallarmé that shaped Machado's aesthetic (Ribbans 1976/77 and 1979; Machado *PrC*, III, 1208–11). But it was also the Bible and the Psalms, popular religious songs, especially the *saeta*, and Spain's mystical writers which served to express a personal theological and aesthetic statement (McDermott

---

[48] See the open letter to Machado which Unamuno published in *Helios*, quoted in G.W. Ribbans, *Niebla y Soledad: Aspectos de Unamuno y Machado* (Madrid: Gredos, 1971), pp. 191–2, where Machado was advised to reject 'el arte por el arte' and write from himself of life, 'sin arte reflexivo' and accept 'la batalla en su terreno', a reference to the campaign of the *Helios* group to 'regenerate' and 'respiritualise' Spain.

1992). A latter-day mystic, Machado sets out on a journey from doubt and darkness to an unstated goal: God, lost love, lost illusions, poetic perfection. And, as with his contemporaries, it is Fray Luis de León, Santa Teresa and San Juan de la Cruz who offer an example. Of the latter he wrote in 1912: 'En San Juan de la Cruz, acaso el más hondo lírico español, la metáfora nunca aparece sino cuando el sentir rebosa [overflows] el cauce lógico, en momentos profundamente emotivos' (*PrC*, III, 1211). But the poetic trajectory of Symbolism, as with Machado's search for an ultimate meaning and faith, also ends in absences; the word cannot capture that absolute goal since the word is no more than a play of differences, constantly shifting. The word cannot be trusted to confer meaning. Powerful ideas overwhelm the creative act; powerful feelings (shades of Shelley and Wordsworth again) are the bedrock of genuine art. 'Sólo el sentimiento es creador. Las ideas se destruyen y pasan' (*PrC*, III, 1482). In 'La desnuda tierra del camino' (XXIII) the reality of this moment of possible epiphany is countered by negative resonances: 'desnuda', 'solitaria', 'umbrosa', 'estéril.' Reality is transmuted into a mirror to the poet's thoughts ('sentimiento'). He can neither communicate with, nor express, the goal of his longings, here expressed in terms of a displaced theology: 'El salmo verdadero / de tenue voz hoy torna / al corazón, y al labio / la palabra quebrada y temblorosa'; never the 'pure' or 'ultimate' word. Appeals to dream and memory (see LXII for example), even as a 'don preclaro' which might lead to self-knowledge, 'con los ojos abiertos' (LXXXIX), represent, in reality, a search for the Word itself, 'algunos lienzos del recuerdo'. Not the Word, merely a 'lienzo', a picture on a canvas, an image among many. As Machado enquires in poem LXXVIII, is the 'magical' world of memory and insight to disperse into nothingness ('el hondo cielo')? Memories of early love evoked in poem VII as a fleeting vision of a shadow on the wall or an elusive scent or his mother and others where he senses a comforting hand or expresses a deep longing (XII and LXXXVII) or seeks to interrogate the beloved (XVI, XXIX and XXXVII), are recalled again here. How do you describe a moving shadow or a perfume? In an echo of the religious doubts of a Quevedo or a Góngora, Machado's final stanza asks if his world of certainties are as certain as he had believed, or are they to end in 'polvo' and 'viento'. The longed-for sacred meaning is muted, expressing itself in broken and hesitant words. The past recalled is dormant, silent, distant. But the final stanza of poem XXIII seems to suggest, in its echo of the end of the Biblical Flood, with a scented breeze bringing new life to the sterile land, a sense of coming union in this mystical 'bendita soledad'. But there is no union, merely the place where it might take place, only its shadow. For San Juan God can be experienced, even embraced. For Machado in this re-writing of the mystical journey, there is only a Symbolist absence, the mere shadow of the desired object. He seeks through symbol, metaphor, metonyms and references not only the spiritual goal for which he longs but also the adequate word to describe and, thus, attain his goal, the 'palabra pura'. The 'alegre leyenda olvidada' of poem VI and the references to glowing eyes (XXIX, XLII and LXIII) are Machado's re-statement of San Juan's search for 'los ojos deseados / Que tengo en mis entrañas dibujadas' of the *Cántico spiritual*. Machado can sense the spiritual power but, as a sceptic, he cannot experience it. His failure in words, the stammer and doubts he expresses across these poems, denote his uncertain hold on belief and, arguably, his sense of poetic impotence, a feeling common in Symbolist practice. This impossible search finds expression in 'Cenit', omitted in *SGOP* in 1907, where Machado interrogates himself as a 'tú'. He creates a contrast between a desired exotic Other and reality. He seeks a reply to 'el enigma del presente [que] te inquieta'. But the fountain – once more a projection of the poet's counter-thoughts – speaks through its 'salterio' (note the religious and Biblical reference again) to offer a Sybiline reply: 'Tu destino / será siempre vagar ¡oh peregrino / del laberinto que tu sueño encierra!' The dream-labyrinth cannot be expressed in adequate language; the poet, now a 'pilgrim' or 'romero' (again the religious register), like the mystic in his journey to illumination, dwells in 'un misterio de sombra' (his 'dark night of the soul'), ensnared in the web of his own sceptical dreams, doomed never to find the way out. Once more he learns, as in poem VI, that there was no former time of revelation. The desired goal is subordinated in a negative response through the objectivisation of his feelings into a *paisaje del alma*. The expression does not move outwards, merely inwards as the poet imposes his 'self' onto the desired landscape and goal. The 'pure' word of revelation cannot be expressed and, thus, experienced. Hence the motif of the 'camino' that leads nowhere, the closed spaces –abandoned gardens, small squares, patios – and Machado's extraordinary 'silences' and self-questioning, all of which end in frustrated meditations and the poet's revision of his own 'dark night of the soul'. The 'saeta popular' stands as a revision of the 'flechas' of San Juan and Santa Teresa. Compare San Juan: 'y haciendo por que mueras / las flechas que recibes / de lo que del Amado en ti concibes' from the *Cántico* (see Ferreres 1964).

Yet the echoes of the mystic literature of the sixteenth century at times is overlaid with the *fin de siglo* fascination with Ancient Greece (Cardwell 2009), one of the few influences of the Decadence we find in Machado's work. In poem XLII he glosses the myth of Artemis, the twin sister of Apollo, who imposes chastity on her acolytes, to create a heterodox combination.[49] At the same time Machado glosses the 'arrows' of Santa Teresa and San Juan as well as the *saeta sevillana*. For all the apparently harmonious setting, the hunt is a 'fugitiva ilusión'. The arrow has struck, but the wound, the 'idea' of a spiritual goal, as in Santa Teresa, cannot be expressed in a 'pure' word. Thus, in poem XXXIII, when the poet enquires of an unstated (thus absent) lover the nature of their love, he evokes a winter landscape in the decaying bullrush, the burnt poppy, the rigid sun and the frozen fountain. While the plant evocations are erotic in a Decadent sense (the classic morbid dying effects of *jardins de supplices* of the *fin de siècle*), the emphasis on immobility and decay also express a typical Decadent spiritual inertia. The frozen fountain, a negation of the mystic's fountain of divine love, as with evocations of a similar type (see 'Tristezas', LXIX) suggest a paralysis of faith, a search caught between hope and pessimism. In 'Sobre la tierra amarga' (XXII) (note the emotive 'amarga' applied to 'tierra' but, of course, it is the poet's own bitterness) Machado evokes, once more, the *camino* motif. Now the road becomes a tortuous labyrinth leading into dark inner spaces and soaring stairs which present past hopes and

---

[49] Artemis, the huntress goddess, was represented in tradition with a bow and a quiver of arrows, dressed in a Doric tunic (*chiton*) and sandals. She wore a crescent moon on her brow and was accompanied by a stag and a bee. This latter symbol appears throughout *SGOP*. See poem XXV and others where the poet evokes the rustle of the *chiton*. For a fuller account see Cardwell, 'Antonio Machado, San Juan de la Cruz y el Neomisticismo', in D. Gareth Walters (ed.), *Estelas en la mar. Essays on the Poetry of Antonio Machado (1875–1939)*, Glasgow Colloquium Papers 2 (Glasgow: University of Glasgow, 1992), pp. 18–37.

memories, 'el don preclaro de evocar los sueños'. While Symbolist in style in the receding planes or spaces, the dumb show of 'figurillas' belongs to the search for revelation. They pass by with smiles at the bend of the path transforming themselves into phantoms forever out of reach. The evocation of hidden spaces and of gardens of delight once more gloss the verses of the Psalms, San Juan, Santa Teresa and Fray Luis. Yet the desired union expressed in these religious sources and their trust in the completion of that union, is never fulfilled. Despite the hope expressed at the end of the poem '¡Tenue rumor de túnicas que pasan ...!' (XXV) (using again the Artemis myth) that 'La hora / de una ilusión se acerca ...', is revealed, in reality, to be just that: an 'ilusión'. The final ellipsis, again the equivalent of a sigh, suggests that the poet must continue to search for some form of faith, religious or poetic. The 'romero' and 'peregrino' poet is not incarcerated, rather trapped in a 'laberinto de espejos' where images and words multiply but never capture the desired object. In poem XXXIV he repeatedly questions the spring dawn, traditional image of rebirth and beginnings, to ask if memories remain 'del hada de tu sueño adamantino'. The adjective 'adamantino' is ambiguous: firm, constant on the one hand, or so unbreakable that he will never understand it in the contrast of 'adamantino' and fragile 'cristal'. The reply is entirely negative, one infinitely postponed: 'Sólo tienen cristal los sueños míos. / Yo no conozco el hada de mis sueños; / ni sé si está mi corazón florido'. The poet is trapped in a prison of fragile refracting glass, a world that is devoid of substance and hope in its infinity of images. The poem ends on a 'Pero...' and a 'si', conditioning what follows. The poet must wait for 'la mañana pura' which will free him from this crystalline world of refracted images. Yet even then that possibility is suspended on a 'quizás'. In other poems the desired union is evoked, as in 'El rojo sol de un sueño' (LXXXIV) where, again at dawn and in a dreamtime, he glimpses the promised goal while recognising that for all the 'luz en sueños' the 'cercano final de tu camino' is subtended on another 'acaso'. As with the *amada* in the *Cántico espiritual* of San Juan, he journeys through a 'campo recién florido y verde' (an echo, too, of Fray Luis and the Song of Songs). Yet, as the conditional subjunctive and the interrogative suggest, '¿quién pudiera / soñar aún largo tiempo en estas pequeñitas / corollas azuladas que manchan la pradera ...?', he has not found the 'ameno huerto deseado' of the *Cántico* and of Fray Luis.[50] He might sense, in his dreams, as in 'El poeta' (XVIII), 'el acento de una palabra divina', but it is only an 'acento' not the 'pure' word. Thus the desire is countered by 'el frío soplo del olvido'. Not the warm breeze of other poems that promises fulfilment, one now cold and not-knowing, oblivion. In the 'huerto ameno', with many echoes again of San Juan, Fray Luis and popular verse, he strives to balance longing ('sed') and disappointment ('dolor') and echoes the Biblical 'Vandidad de vanidades'. Yet there is a glimpse of a '¡Noche de amor! (another echo of the mystics) but, once more, it is undermined by 'la mala tristeza' of another night when he, the poet, becomes a 'poor player' declaiming his doubts and desires before deserted, silent and empty galleries, the haunting crystalline world of his imagination casting prismatic images into an infinity of doubt. While the demons of thought offer the elusive gardens of delight of yesteryear, a time that never was, he senses a deceit: the beauty of the longed-for past is a false springtime, autumn fruits are eaten by the ravening worm. While the poet struggles to recapture youthful illusions he can only discover 'la humilde flor de la melancolía', another Decadent motif. Dreams offer only a seesaw of hope and disillusion in this secular mystical journey.[51] The 'demonio de mi sueño' is also 'el ángel más hermoso'. But, unlike San Juan's and Santa Teresa's quests through caves of darkness, for Machado the angel-demon lights up 'la honda cripta del alma' and the

---

[50] Here, and in many other poems of *SGOP* and *Campos de Castilla*, we witness Machado's eye for natural elements, which aspect is in tune with that of other young writers of the period, another break with the poetry of the late nineteenth century. See for example poem L, 'Acaso'. I suggest this love of nature was formed in Machado from excursions into the countryside led by Giner de los Ríos of the Institución Libre during his school days. See A. Rodríguez Forteza, *La naturaleza y Antonio Machado* (San Juan, Puerto Rico: Ediciones Cordillera, 1965); Emilio Orozco, 'Antonio Machado en el camino. Notas de un tema central de su poesía', in *Paisaje y sentimientos de la naturaleza en la poesía española* (Madrid: Prensa Española, 1968); and Reyes Vila-Belda, 'La visión institucionista del paisaje en Antonio Machado', in Domènech, *Hoy es siempre todavía* (2006), pp. 198–229.

[51] Compare this to and fro between hope and despair with the statement of Azorín, Machado's friend, in *Diario de un enfermo* (1901). The diary is presented as that of 'un angustiado artista', 'nostálgico de ideal'! (1901, I, 691). In *Antonio Azorín*, a year later, he wrote 'La fe nos hace vivir, sin ella la vida es insoportable ... ¡Y es lo triste que la fe se pierda! ¡Y se pierda con ella el sosiego, la resignación, la perfecta ataraxia del espíritu que se contempla rodeado de dolores irremediables, necesarios!' (1902, I, 889–900).

poet is forced to advance into his questing mind to a fearful place filled with dread (LXIII). Rarely does 'la voz querida' appear to give direction. But, as in 'Campo' (LXXX), he enters a symbolic 'dark night of the soul', evoked in fading light, described as cooling embers and withered leaves, only to glimpse, far off, 'los álamos de oro, / lejos, la sombra del amor'. Once more a restatement of Greek myth, as we shall see, joined with the landscapes of Spain's mystical tradition.

Thus the labyrinthine journey through these dark or prismatic galleries, crypts and tortuous paths and stairs, Machado's re-writing of the mystical journey, swerves from San Juan and Santa Teresa to Greek myth. The 'álamos de oro', in reality poplars bathed in evening light on a mountainside (possibly from walks in the Guadarrama or near Soria and, thus, a late poem), become a potent symbol associated with the Ancient Greek mythical place of Parnassus where the Muses sport amid trees laden with golden fruit sacred to Apollo, God of Poetry and Light. Greek myth supplements the mystic tradition where the love of God becomes the 'love' of the pure Word offered by the Muses and Apollo. Thus Machado expresses his Symbolist search and his spiritual search in both pagan and Christian tradition: the Muses' 'inspiration' and St John's 'In the beginning was the Word'. Poem XCI, for example, bears as its central motif the same 'árboles de oro'. The frequent mention of scarlet or golden fruit is a recurring symbol in *SGOP*. Elsewhere, the golden light of Helicon is offered as a poetic goal but transmuted into the threshold to 'la tierra verde y santa y florecida de [sus] sueños', in an uncanny echo of the Psalms. And these symbols of the site of poetic and spiritual inspiration, the Muses and Apollo and the mystical progress, are the means whereby he seeks some consoling belief: the search, as with San Juan, for a means to express what appears inexpressible, the search for the adequate word. Is what he writes his authentic voice or is it the babble of a clown or 'poor player'? In a re-writing of San Juan's colloquy between the Amado and the Amada in poem XXXVII, where he addresses his own Symbolist 'dark night of the soul', his 'noche amiga, amada vieja', he seeks reassurance of his own sincerity, his own 'true' voice, amid a dumb show of his sorrows: 'si son mías las lágrimas que vierto'. But his female interlocutor cannot vouch for his sincerity nor his secret, even though she has visited 'la honda gruta / donde fabrica su cristal mi sueño'. She can give witness to the sincerity of 'las almas cuando lloran / y escucho su hondo rezo, / humilde y solitario, / ese que llamas salmo verdadero'. But in the depths of the poet's soul his lament is uncertain. In this interior search she finds the poet wandering in 'un borroso / laberinto de espejos'. We note the religious cast of this dialogue in 'rezo' and 'salmo' interwoven with the Machado motif of a hall of distorting mirrors, prismatic walls of glass reflecting, repeating and refracting his image (his word) striving to proceed to a desired goal but one always projected to infinity, the very heart of Symbolist poetics. In many ways this type of evocation is a recasting of the mystical journey through the 'dark night of the soul', in the sense of abandonment and the desire for final union. At the same time Machado employs the Symbolist aesthetic of internally infolding frames and spaces since his ministry is to find the adequate word for his new messianic message. The poet/priest must express the 'Word', the equivalent of the Symbolist union with God. The search for a spiritual 'self' and the search for the adequate word to define the relationship between seeker and goal become intertwined. It is always, in a possible echo of Mallarmé's 'Je dis une fleur' [I say 'a flower'] which rises from the unconscious mind ('oubli'), 'una flor que quiere echar su aroma al viento' (LXI), marks a desire ('quiere') that seeks to supervene reality and lead to a secular form of speculative, rather than dogmatic, Christian theology. In this aptly named poem – 'Introducción' – an important poetic manifesto for the *guerra literaria*, he evokes once more the idea of a 'verdad divina' as he seeks 'el misterio'. Only the poet can engage in this search in the 'galerías / sin fondo', symbol of the imaginative mind, evoked in the traditional image of the bee and honey, another symbol taken from Santa Teresa's *Moradas primeras* of the *Castillo interior*, which Machado uses and re-uses in 'Anoche cuando dormía' (LIX), along with, in other poems, the popular image of the orchard implied or stated. He also echoes, here, San Juan's *Cantar del alma que se huelga de conocer a Dios por fe*. And also, more significantly, with images of war: 'batalla', 'el fuerte arnés de guerra'. Yet there remains the sense of constant effort undermined by 'el enemigo espejo', the world of Symbolist refracting glass. But here, too, we return to Machado's letter to Jiménez in 1903 to the effect that 'es necesario afrontar una gran lucha contra la ignoble chusma [rabble] nutrida de la bazofia ambiente [an ambience of pigswill]. Pero hay que luchar sabiendo que los fuertes somos nosotros ... Yo protesto ...' This sentiment is a secular re-statement of a spiritual (*neo-místico*) journey when he argues that personal anguish can form a part of the general 'guerra' of the young writers to regenerate their fellow countrymen. In another letter to Jiménez in 1913, mentioning Azorín's *Castilla* and 'el problema de nuestra patria', Machado concludes, the letter: 'En fin, trabajemos pacientemente nuestras armas [that is, poetry]. Pero, al fin, es preciso ir a la guerra' (*PrC*, III, 1519).The poet needs to 'pray' and 'sing', that is, write authentic verses and discover the 'salmo verdadero' since he is, as the Krausists, Darío, Unamuno and others claimed, a 'sacerdote' and a 'redentor'. But poetry is also a weapon of war against Spain's backwardness. In this introductory poem he echoes the force of the spiritual campaign he shared with others and with the *Helios* group: 'Poeta, con el alma / atenta al hondo cielo, / en la cruel batalla / o en el tranquilo huerto, / la nueva miel labramos /con los dolores viejos'. Former doubts and anguish can form the seedbed for progress. Here in an echo of Darío's 'Atrio' to Jiménez's 1900 *Ninfeas* – '¿Tienes, joven amigo, ceñida la coraza / Para empezar valiente la divina pelea?' – Fray Luis's version of the *Beatus ille* and the Biblical assertion that 'Out of the strong comes forth sweetness', Machado suggests, as he had written to Jiménez, that the expression of spiritual doubt and the pursuit of the consequences of that doubt in the search for meaning and purpose was a vital part of the generational consensus to re-generate the nation spiritually. Scepticism and spiritual doubt were, for these men, and Machado, an enabling condition for a personal and a national salvation. Such is the import of poem LX where the image of the bee and honey recur in the poet's 'colmenar de sueños' as does the image of the dry fountain. But the reply to this apparent sterility is positive: his 'corazón', his vital 'self', 'Está despierto, despierto. / No duerme ni sueña, mira, / los claros ojos abiertos, / señas lejanas y escucha / a orillas del gran silencio'. The search for a spiritual goal, for national redemption, for self, the search for the adequate word to express that faith, all come together in these *neo-místico* and Symbolist statements. But, nevertheless the 'señas' are 'lejanas'. Now and again he finds a temporary faith for the artist in a revelatory dream (his version of the mystic illumination) in a '¡bendita ilusión!' as he terms it in poem LIX. But it remains an 'ilusión'. He re-works the theological virtues of faith, hope and charity, San Juan's 'Noche oscura' and 'Llama de amor viva' and a dream of God, another 'bendita ilusión'. Yet in other poems he swerves to evocations of the self-reflecting and infinite crystalline galleries and voices which tempt now with hope and promise, now with disillusion. But he cannot decide: is he a 'true' poet or a 'poor player'? The search for faith and meaning is combined with the search for the Word itself,[52] one that can express fully that ultimate goal. Is the voice (word) he writes a true one, authentic, reliable ('la voz tuya') or is it the worn utterances of a tired and ageing actor, once capable of enthralling with his message, now a grotesque figure of opprobrium speaking in tired rote and cliché. This poetic trajectory becomes the symbol of the search for an ever-absent theology. Poetry becomes a new form of a religion in the true sense, rather than in the sense the *gente vieja* attributed to institutional theology in their attacks on the new generation. Machado sought to create a basis for faith in poetry; for himself and for his fellow Spaniards. But rather than creating verses which expressed an absolute Idea (God, a centre of faith, an Other, a Being) these poems, expressing doubt, scepticism and disillusion, create a countervailing force, an Absence where all paths –the *caminos*, crypts, caverns, *galerías* – lead to distant impossible horizons or into constantly reflecting walls of mirrors. Counter to the strident appeal to national, imperial and patriotic ideals of the previous decades, Machado offers a countervailing message of reality: doubt challenged by hope, faith by scepticism, introspection by altruism. Machado is one of the prominent *neo-místico* poets of his generation and of the *Helios* group dedicated to the regeneration of the nation and, at the same time, one of Spain's consummate Symbolists, the poet of absences and suggestion. *SGOP* marks, then, a major landmark in the development and regeneration of the lyric at the beginning of the twentieth century.

---

[52] Beneath the Symbolist obsession with the ultimate Word lies, of course, the opening of the Gospel of St John: 'In the beginning was the Word'.

Select bibliography

Acosta, Ángel / Vázquez, Manuel A. (1990), 'Demófilo, Antonio Machado y la poesía popular', in *Antonio Machado hoy*, I, 151–60.

Aguilar, Encarnación (1989) (ed.), *Antonio Machado y Núñez. Páginas escogidas* (Sevilla, Serie de Publicaciones del Excmo Ayuntamiento de Sevilla).

Aguirre, José María (1973), *Antonio Machado, poeta simbolista* (Madrid: Taurus).

Alarcón Sierra, A. (2009), '"A orillas del gran silencio": el ciclo simbolista de Antonio Machado', in Antonio Jiménez Millán (ed.), *Antonio Machado: Laberinto de espejos* (Málaga: Junta de Andalucía Consejería de Cultura – Centro Andaluz de las Letras), pp. 241–63.

Albornoz, Aurora de (1968), *La presencia de Miguel de Unamuno en Antonio Machado* (Madrid: Gredos).

Alonso, Dámaso (1965), 'Fuente y jardín en la poesía de Antonio Machado', *Poesía española contemporánea* (Madrid: Gredos), pp. 130–47.

Alonso Montero, Xesús (1989), 'Antonio Machado y Álvarez ("Demófilo") y la poesía popular gallega', *Ínsula*, 506–7, 7–8.

Antonio Machado hoy (1990), ed. Jorge Urrutia. Actas del Congreso Internacional Conmemorativo del Cincuentenario de la muerte de Antonio Machado (Sevilla: Alfar), 4 vols.

Baker, Armand F. (1985), *El pensamiento religioso y filosófico de Antonio Machado*, Servicio de Publicaciones del Excmo Ayuntamiento de Sevilla (Sevilla: Imprenta Escandón).

Baltanás, Enrique (2006a), 'Los orígenes de la Escuela Popular de Sabiduría Superior: la idea de pueblo en Antonio Machado y Álvarez', in Domènech, *Hoy es siempre*, pp. 11–64.

—— (2006b), *Los Machado. Una familia, dos siglos de cultura española* (Madrid: Fundación José Manuel de Lara).

Baroja, Pío (1946–51), *Obras Completas* (Madrid: Biblioteca Nueva).

Berlin, Isaiah (1996), *The Sense of Reality. Studies in Ideas and their History* (London: Chatto & Windus).

Blanco Aguinaga, C. (1970), *Juventud del 98* (Madrid: Siglo Veintiuno de España Editores).

Blasco, Javier (1981), *La poética de Juan Ramón Jiménez: contexto, desarrollo y sistema* (Salamanca: Universidad de Salamanca), pp. 79–87.

—— (2000), 'El "98" que nunca existió', in Joseph Harrison and Alan Hoyle (eds), *Spain's 1898 Crisis. Regenerationism, modernism and post-colonialism* (Manchester: Manchester University Press), pp. 121–31.

Bousoño, C. (1952), *Teoría de la expresión poética* (Madrid: Gredos).

Brotherston, J.G. (1964), 'Antonio Machado y Álvarez and Positivism', *Bulletin of Hispanic Studies*, XLI, 223–9.

Cacho Viu, Vicente (1962 and reprint 2010), *La Institución Libre de Enseñanza (Orígenes y etapa universitaria 1860–1881)* (Madrid: Editorial Rialp / Editorial Fundación Albéniz).

Cardwell, Richard A. (1972), Ricardo Gil, *La caja de música, critical edition and introduction*, Exeter Hispanic Texts (Exeter: University of Exeter Press).

—— (1974), 'Juan Ramón Jiménez and the Decadence', *Revista de Letras* (Mayagüez, Puerto Rico), 23–4, 291–342.

—— (1981), '*Modernismo frente a noventayocho:* The Case of Juan Ramón Jiménez' (1899–1900), in *Estudios sobre Juan Ramón Jiménez* (Puerto Rico: University of Mayagüez), pp. 119–41.

—— (1984a), 'Myths Ancient and Modern: *Modernismo frente a noventayocho* and the Search for Spain', in Richard A. Cardwell (ed.), *Essays in Honour of R. B. Tate from his Colleagues and Pupils* (Nottingham: University of Nottingham Monographs in the Humanities), pp. 9–21.

—— (1984b), Francisco A. de Icaza, *Efímeras & Lejanías, critical edition and introduction*, Exeter Hispanic Texts (Exeter: University of Exeter Press).

—— (1985a), 'A Symbolist poem of Antonio Machado' in *Readings in Spanish and Portuguese Poetry for Geoffrey Connell* (Glasgow: University of Glasgow), pp. 3–15.

—— (1985b), 'Juan Ramón, Ortega y los intelectuales', *Hispanic Review*, 53, 329–50.

—— (1987), 'Cómo se escribe un poema simbolista: el caso de Antonio Machado', *Actas del seminario internacional. El modernismo español e hispanoamericano* (Córdoba: Diputación de Córdoba), pp. 321–36.

—— (1989a), 'Symbolist Solipsism: Musing on Mirrors and Myths', *Language and Literature – Theory and Practice: A Tribute to Walter Grauberg* (Nottingham: University of Nottingham Monographs in the Humanities), pp. 83–100.

—— (1989b), 'Beyond the Mirror and the Lamp: Symbolist Frames and Spaces', *Romance Quarterly*, 36, 2, 267–72.

—— (1989c), 'Introducción' to Manuel Machado, *Antología* (Sevilla: Servicios de Publicaciones de la Excmo Ayuntamiento de Sevilla).

—— (1989d), 'Antonio Machado: ¿Modernista, noventayochista o poeta finisecular?', *Ínsula* 505-7, 16-18.

—— (1990), 'Mirrors and Myths: Antonio Machado and the Search for Self', *Romance Studies*, 16, 31-42.

—— (1991), 'Degeneration, Discourse and Differentiation. Modernismo frente a noventayocho Reconsidered', in *Critical Essays on the Literatures of Spain and Spanish America. Anejo, Anales de la literatura española contemporánea*. Society for Spanish and Spanish American Studies (Boulder, CO: University Press of Colorado), pp. 29-46.

—— (1992), 'Antonio Machado, San Juan de la Cruz y el Neomisticismo', in D. Gareth Walters (ed.), *Estelas en la mar. Essays on the Poetry of Antonio Machado (1875-1939)*, Glasgow Colloquium Papers 2 (Glasgow: University of Glasgow), pp. 18-37.

—— (1993), '"Una hermandad de trabajadores espirituales": Nueva aproximación al enfrentismo y a la definición del modernismo', in Richard A. Cardwell and B. J. McGuirk (eds), *¿Qué es el modernismo? Nueva encuesta. Nuevas lecturas*. Society for Spanish and Spanish American Studies (Boulder, CO: University Press of Colorado), pp. 159-92.

—— (1994), 'Al-Andalus y Andalucía: historia y cultura en el modernismo español', in Ralph Penny (ed.), *Actas del I Congreso Anglo-Hispano*, tomo III (Madrid: Castalia), pp. 81-91.

—— (1997a), 'Espejo y sueño: la práctica simbolista en España; in *La metáfora en la poesía hispánica (1885-1936)*. Actas del simposio celebrado en la Universidad de Copenhague, 25 y 26 de setiembre de 1996 (Sevilla: Editorial Alfar), pp. 19-35.

—— (1997b)'Los Machado y Juan Ramón Jiménez "en el 98": buscando nuevas trazas por las ciudades muertas y las sendas abandonadas', in José-Carlos Mainer y Jordi Gracia (eds), *En el 98 (los nuevos escritores)* (Madrid: Visor), pp. 137-57.

—— (2000a), 'Romanticism, *Modernismo* and *Noventa y ocho*: The Creation of a *Poesía nacional*', *Bulletin of Spanish Studies*, LXXXII, 3-4, 471-93.

—— (2000b), 'Juan Ramón Jiménez y el Desastre de 1898', in *Ensayos en Honor de José Martínez Cachero* (Oviedo: Universidad de Oviedo), II, pp. 335-56.

—— (2000c), 'The War of the Wor(l)ds: Symbolist Decadent Literature and the Discourses of Power in Finisecular Spain', in Patrick McGuiness (ed.), *Symbolism, Decadence and the Fin de siècle. French and European Perspectives*. (Exeter: University of Exeter Press), pp. 225-43.

—— (2002), '"La poesía moderna, modernísima, poesía, quizás, del futuro". Los orígenes del simbolismo en España', *Anales de Literatura española*, 15, 27-53.

—— (2006), 'Antonio Machado, la Institución y el idealismo finisecular', in Jordi Domènech, *Hoy es siempre*, I, pp. 65–86.

—— (2007), 'Juan Ramón Jiménez y la tradición pastoral: la búsqueda de una edad dorada', in Ángel Esteban (coordinador), *Darío a diario. Rubén y el modernismo en las dos orillas* (Granada: Universidad de Granada), pp. 373–400.

—— (2009), '"Amo más que la Grecia de los griegos / la Grecia de Francia": Ancient Greece in the Spanish Lyric 1870–1910', *Studi Ispanici*, XXXIV, 95–111.

—— (2012), '¿Radicalismo político o estética radical?', in Jochen Mecke (coordinador), *Discursos de 98. Albores españoles de una modernidad europea* (Madrid-Frankfurt am Main: Iberamericana-Vervuert), pp. 101–24.

—— (2013), '"Un monarca de la bohemia": Alejandro Sawa, la *gente nueva* y el momento finisecular. Patologías y semblanzas', *Hispanic Journal*, 34, 2, 29–44.

Carr, R. (1966), *Spain 1808–1975* (Oxford: Clarendon).

Carvalho-Neto, Paulo de (1975), *La influencia del folklore en Antonio Machado* (Madrid: Ediciones Demófilo).

Casalduero, Joaquín (1964), 'Machado, poeta institucionista y masón', *La Torre*, XII, 45–6, 99–110.

Celma Valero, María Pilar (1991), *Literatura y periodismo en las revistas del fin de siglo. Estudio e índices (1888–1907)* (Madrid: Ediciones Júcar).

Celma Valero, María Pilar and Blasco, Javier (eds) (1981), *Manuel Machado, La guerra literaria*, Bitácora (Madrid: Narcea).

Cernuda, L. (1957), *Estudios sobre poesía española contemporánea* (Madrid: Guadarrama).

Correa, Amelina (2006), 'Antonio Machado en el ámbito del modernismo andaluz', in Domènech, *Hoy es siempre todavía,* pp. 87–138.

Domènech, Jordi (coordinador) (2006), *Hoy es siempre todavía. Curso Internacional sobre Antonio Machado* (Córdoba: Ayuntamiento de Córdoba / Sevilla: Renacimiento).

—— (2009a), *Antonio Machado. Epistolario (*Barcelona: Octaedro).

—— (2009b), 'Variaciones en torno a los escritos dispersos de Antonio Machado', in Antonio Jiménez Millán (ed.), *Antonio Machado: Laberinto de espejos (*Málaga: Junta de Andalucía Consejería de Cultura – Centro Andaluz de las Letras), pp. 325–39.

DuPont, Denise (2013), 'Krausism and Modernism', *Hispanic Journal*, 34, 2, 13–28.

Ferreres, Rafael (1964), 'La flecha alegórica con que hiere el Amor' in *Los límites del modernismo y del 98* (Madrid: Taurus).

—— (1975), *Verlaine y los modernistas españoles* (Madrid: Gredos), pp. 129–54.
Flitter, Derek (1991), *Romantic Traditionalism: Directions in Literary Theory and Criticism in Spain (1814–1850)* (Cambridge: Cambridge University Press).
—— (1992), *Spanish Romantic Literary Theory and Criticism* (Cambridge: Cambridge University Press).
—— (1993), 'La misión regeneradora de la literatura: del romanticismo al modernismo pasando por Krause', in Richard A. Cardwell and B. J. McGuirk (eds), *¿Qué es el modernismo? Nueva encuesta. Nuevas lecturas*, Society of Spanish and Spanish-American Studies (Boulder: University of Colorado), pp. 127–46.
Fogelquist, Donald F. (1955), '*Helios*, voz de un renacimiento hispánico', *Revista Iberoamericana*, XX, 291–99.
Fox, E. Inman (1976), *La crisis intelectual del 98* (Madrid: Cuadernos para el diálogo).
García Blanco, Manuel (1965), *En torno a Unamuno* (Madrid: Taurus).
Gicovate, B (1967), 'La evolución poética de Antonio Machado', in *Ensayos sobre poesía hispánica* (Mexico: Caraco).
Gil Novales, Alberto (1970), *Antonio Machado* (Barcelona: 'Testigos del siglo XX', núm. 16).
Goldberg, Brian (2007), *The Lake Poets and Professional Identity* (Cambridge: Cambridge University Press).
Gómez Montero, Javier (1990), 'La recepción de la poesía francesa contemporánea en *Soledades. Galerías. Otros poemas* (Una revisión bajo el enfoque de la intertextualidad)', in *Antonio Machado hoy*, III, pp. 9–32.
González, Beatriz, Rodríguez, Santiago and Cardwell, Richard A. (2008), 'The Reception of Shelley in Spain', in Susanna Schmid and Michael Rossington (eds), *The Reception of P. B. Shelley in Europe* (London/New York: Continuum), pp. 97–110.
Grass, Roland and Risley, William R. (eds) (1979), *Waiting for Pegasus: Studies of the Presence of Symbolism and Decadence in Hispanic Letters,* An Essays in Literature Book (Macomb, IL).
Gullón, R. (1949), 'La unidad en la obra de Antonio Machado', *Ínsula*, 40, 1 and 16.
—— (1958), *Las secretas galerías de Antonio Machado* (Madrid: Taurus).
—— (1959), 'Cartas de Antonio Machado a Juan Ramón Jiménez'; 'Relaciones amistosas ...'; 'Prosa y verso de Machado a Jiménez'; 'Prosa y verso de Jiménez a Machado', *La Torre*, VII, 25, 159–224.
—— (1960), Relaciones amistosas y literarias entre Antonio Machado y Juan

Ramón Jiménez', in *Estudios sobre Juan Ramón Jiménez* (Buenos Aires: Losada), pp. 53–68.

—— (1970), *Una poética para Antonio Machado* (Madrid: Gredos).

Gutiérrez Carbajo, Francisco (2006), 'La poesía de tipo popular en Antonio Machado', in Domènech, *Hoy es siempre todavía*, pp. 254–78.

Gutiérrez García, M. (2008), 'El cuervo de E.A. Poe en 'Nevermore' y 'Mai piú', dos poemas de Antonio Machado', *Cuadernos Hispanoamericanos*, 30, 55–68.

Havard, Robert (2007), *The Spanish Eye: Painters and Poets of Spain* (Woodborough: Tamesis).

Heydl Cortínez, Cecelia (1995), 'Giner de los Ríos, el maestro de unos poemas de Unamuno, Antonio Machado y en la prosa de Jiménez', *Hispanic Journal*, núm. 2, 339–49.

Horànyi, Màtyàs (1975), *Las dos Soledades de Antonio Machado* (Budapest: Akadémiai Kiadó).

Ilie, Paul (1962), 'Verlaine and Machado: the aesthetic role of time', *Comparative Literature*, XIV, 261–5.

Jiménez, María Dolores and Agudelo Herrero, Joaquín (1990), 'La personalidad y la obra científica de Antonio Machado y Núñez (1812–1896)', in *Antonio Machado hoy*, I, 167–90.

Jiménez Millán, Antonio (ed). (2009), *Antonio Machado: Laberinto de espejos* (Málaga: Junta de Andalucía Consejería de Cultura – Centro Andaluz de las Letras).

Johnson, Philip G. (2002), *The Power of Paradox in the Work of the Spanish Poet Antonio Machado* (Lewiston, NY: Mellen).

Lipp, Solomon (1985), *Francisco Giner de los Ríos. A Spanish Socrates* (Waterloo, Ontario: Wilfrid Laurier University).

Litvak, Lily (1998), *Imágenes y textos. Estudios sobre literatura y pintura, 1849–1936* (Amsterdam-Atlanta: Rodopi).

López Álvarez, Juan (1996), *El krausismo en los escritos de Antonio Machado y Álvarez* (Cádiz: Servicio de Publicaciones de la Universidad de Cádiz).

López Morillas, Juan (ed.) (1969), Francisco Giner de los Ríos, *Ensayos* (Madrid: Alianza Editorial).

—— (1972), *Hacia el 98: literatura, sociedad, ideología* (Barcelona: Ariel) 'Una crisis de la conciencia española: krausismo y religión', pp. 119–59 (Essay of 1966).

—— (1981), *The Krausist Movement and Ideological Change in Spain 1854–1874*, Cambridge Iberian and Latin American Studies (Cambridge: Cambridge University Press).

Lozano, Miguel A. (1990), 'La "Ciudad Muerta" en la poesía de Antonio

Machado', in *Antonio Machado hoy*, I, pp. 465–76.

—— (2006), '"El cristal y el espejo". Azorín visto por Antonio Machado', in Domènech, *Hoy es siempre todavía*, pp. 254–78.

Machado, Antonio (1975 and 1998), *Soledades. Galerías. Otros poemas*, ed. G.W. Ribbans (Madrid: Editorial Labor; Madrid: Cátedra).

Macrì, Oreste (ed.) (1988), *Poesía y prosa*, Tomo III, *Prosa completa* (Madrid: Espasa-Calpe / Fundación Antonio Machado).

Mainer, J-C. (ed.) (1974), *La crisis de fin de siglo: Ideología y literatura* (Barcelona).

—— (ed.) (1995), *Antonio Machado. Poesía (*Barcelona: Vicens Vives).

—— and Jordi Gracia (eds) (1997), *En el 98 (Los nuevos escritores)* (Madrid: Visor Libros / Fundación Duques de Soria).

March-Martul, Kathleen N. (1982)'Análisis estilístico de "El viajero", de Antonio Machado', *Revista de Estudios Hispánicos*, 16, pp. 453–65.

Mattauch, H. (2003), 'Las "galerías" de Antonio Machado: origen y evolución de una metáfora central de su poesía', *Revista de Literatura*, 129, 225–35.

McDermott, Patricia (1992), 'Songlines of the Dreamtime on a Map of Misreading (An Unscientific Meditation on the *Soledades* of Antonio Machado for the Evening of Palm Sunday 1989)', in D. Gareth Walters (ed.), *Estelas en la mar. Essays on the Poetry of Antonio Machado (1875–1939),* Glasgow Colloquium Papers 2 (Glasgow: University of Glasgow), pp. 1–17.

Meyers, Janet (1954), 'El recuerdo, las galerías y el espejo en las primeras poesías de Antonio Machado', *Revista Hispánica Moderna*, XX, 1–13.

Mills, S. (2009), 'Reflective Mind-Reading: Theory of Mind and the Search for Self in Antonio Machado's *Soledades*', *Hispania* (Ann Arbor), 94, 589–602.

Morales, C.J. (2000), 'Dos versiones del modernismo: la conciencia del tiempo en Rubén Darío y Antonio Machado', *Revista de Literatura*, 62, 107–29.

Oringer, N.R. (2001), 'Superseding Temporality in Antonio Machado's *Soledades*: a Quest for the Golden Age', *Bulletin of Hispanic Studies* (Glasgow), 78, 335–59.

O'Riordan, Patricia (1973), '*Helios*, Revista del modernismo (1903–1904)', *Abaco*, 4, 57–150.

Orozco, Emilio (1968), 'Antonio Machado en el camino. Notas de un tema central de su poesía', in *Paisaje y sentimientos de la naturaleza en la poesía española* (Madrid: Prensa Española).

Palley, Julian (1975), 'Las secretas galerías de Antonio Machado', *Cuadernos Americanos*, XXXI, 210–26.

Paniagua, D. (1964), '*Helios* (1903–1904). Los hombres de *Helios*', *Punta Europa*, 94–5, 21–33.

Pérez Ferrero, M. (1947), *Vida de Antonio Machado y Manuel* (Madrid: Rialp).
Pérez Gago, S. (1984), *Razón, 'sueño' y realidad en Antonio Machado* (Salamanca: Universidad de Salamanca).
Pineda Novo, Daniel (1990), 'La familia de Machado en la Sevilla de la época', in *Antonio Machado hoy*, I, pp. 191–200.
—— (1991), *Antonio Machado y Álvarez. Vida y obra del primer flamencólogo español* (Madrid: Editorial Cinterco y Fundación Andaluza de Flamenco).
Predmore, Michael P. (1974–75), 'The Nostalgia for Paradise and the Dilemma of Solipsism in the Early Poetry of Antonio Machado', *Revista Hispánica Moderna*, XXXVIII, 23–39.
—— (1978), 'The Vision of an Imprisoned and Moribund Society in the *Soledades, Galerías y otros poemas* [sic] of Antonio Machado', *Ideologies and Literature*, II, 8, 14–30.
—— (1989), 'La herencia andaluza en las *Soledades* de Antonio Machado', *Ínsula*, 506-7, 1 and 12.
Ramsden, H. (ed.) (1966), Martínez Ruiz, *La ruta de don Quijote* (Manchester: Manchester University Press).
——(1974a), 'The Spanish "Generation of 1898"', reprinted from the *Bulletin of the John Rylands University Library of Manchester*, 56, 2, 463–91; 57, 1, 167–95 (Manchester: John Rylands University of Manchester).
—— (1974b), *The 1898 Movement in Spain* (Manchester: Manchester University Press).
Regueiro Salgado, Begoña (2010), *La poesía del segundo romanticismo español* (Madrid: Fundación Universitaria Española).
Reyrègne, F. (2000), 'Antonio Machado, deseo y frustración', in Patrick Collard and Eric Storm, *Cambio de siglo. Ideas, mentalidades, sensibilidades en España hacia 1900* (Amsterdam/Atlanta: Rodopi).
Ribbans, G.W. (1957a), 'Machado and Unamuno', *Bulletin of Hispanic Studies*, XXXIV, 10–28.
—— (1957b), 'La influencia de Verlaine en Antonio Machado', *Cuadernos Hispanoamericanos*, XXI, 91–92, 180–201.
—— (1968/69), 'Nuevas precisiones sobre la influencia de Verlaine en Antonio Machado', *Filología* (Buenos Aires), XIII, 295–303.
—— (1971), *Niebla y Soledad: Aspectos de Unamuno y Machado* (Madrid: Gredos).
—— (1972), 'Recaptured Memory in Juan Ramón Jiménez and Antonio Machado', in Nigel Glendinning (ed.), *Studies in Modern Spanish Literature and Art presented to Helen F. Grant* (London: Tamesis), pp. 149–61.
—— (1975 and 1998), *Antonio Machado. Soledades. Galerías. Otros poemas* (Madrid: Editorial Labor). An enlarged edition (Madrid: Cátedra).

—— (1976/77), 'Antonio Machado y Mallarmé', *Revista Hispánica Moderna*, XIX–XX, 4, 83–97.
—— (1979), 'Antonio Machado's Attitude to Symbolism', in Roland Grass and William R. Risley (eds), *Waiting for Pegasus: Studies of the Presence of Symbolism and Decadence in Hispanic Letters*, An Essays in Literature Book (Macomb, IL), pp. 39–56.
—— (2006), 'Antonio Machado: de los 'paisajes del alma' al 'alma del paisaje'', in Domènech, *Hoy es siempre todavía*, pp. 139–72.
Rodríguez Forteza, A. (1965), *La naturaleza y Antonio Machado* (San Juan, Puerto Rico: Ediciones Cordillera).
Romero López, Dolores (2006), *Antonio Machado, Soledades* (Exeter: Exeter University Press).
—— (2013), 'El trasfondo ocultista del cuervo: desde su simbolismo a los topoi modernistas', *Ilu. Revista de Ciencias de la Religión*, 18, 201–18.
Ros, Xon (2010), 'Metamorphic Imagination in Antonio Machado's "El poeta"', *Hispanic Research Journal*, 11, 4, September, 291–307.
Ruiz Ramón, F. (1962a), 'En torno al sentido de "*El espejo de sus sueños*" en la poesía de Antonio Machado', *Revista de Literatura*, XXII, 43–4, 74–83.
—— (1962b), 'El tema del camino en la poesía de Antonio Machado', *Cuadernos Hispanoamericanos*, LI, núm. 151, 52–76.
Sánchez Trigueros, Antonio and Cardwell, Richard A. (1996), José Sánchez Rodríguez, *Alma andaluza (Poesías completas)* (Granada: Universidad de Granada).
Segre, Cesare (1970), *Crítica bajo control* (Barcelona: Planeta).
Sesé, Bernard (1980), *Antonio Machado (1875–1939). El hombre. El poeta. El escritor*, 2 vols (Madrid: Gredos).
Shaw, D.L. (1972), 'Romántico', in Hans Eichner (ed.), *Romanticism. The History of a Word*, (Toronto: University Press), pp. 341–71.
Tully, Carol (2007), *Johann Nikolaus Böhl von Faber (1770–1836): A German Romantic in Spain* (Cardiff: University of Wales Press).
Unamuno, Miguel de (1958), *Obras completas* (Madrid: Afrodisio Aguado).
Urbano, Manuel (1982), *El cante jondo en Antonio Machado* (Madrid: Ediciones Demófilo).
Vila-Belda, Reyes (2004), *Antonio Machado. Poeta de lo nimio* (Madrid: Visor Libros).
—— (2006), 'La visión institucionista del paisaje en Antonio Machado', in Domènech, *Hoy es siempre todavía*, pp. 198–229.
Walters, D. Gareth and Round, Nicholas (eds) (1992), *Estelas en la mar. Essays on the Poetry of Antonio Machado (1875–1939)*, Glasgow Colloquium Papers 2 (Glasgow: University of Glasgow).

Wilcox, John C. (1985), 'The Rhetoric of Existential Anguish in a Poem (LXXVII) of Antonio Machado', *Hispanic Review*, 53, 163–80.

Young, Howard T. (1980), *The Line in the Margin: Juan Ramón Jiménez and his Readings in Blake, Shelley and Yeats* (Madison: University of Wisconsin Press).

Zardoya, Concha (1961), 'El cristal y el espejo en la poesía de Antonio Machado', in *Poesía española contemporánea* (Madrid: Guadarrama).

Zubiría, R. de (1955), *La poesía de Antonio Machado* (Madrid: Gredos).

Soledades. Galerías. Otros poemas

Soledades

I

(EL VIAJERO)

　　Está en la sala familiar, sombría,
y entre nosotros, el querido hermano
que en el sueño infantil de un claro día
vimos partir hacia un país lejano.

　　Hoy tiene ya las sienes plateadas,
un gris mechón sobre la angosta frente;
y la fría inquietud de sus miradas
revela un alma casi toda ausente.

　　Deshójanse las copas otoñales
del parque mustio y viejo.
La tarde, tras los húmedos cristales,
se pinta, y en el fondo del espejo.

　　El rostro del hermano se ilumina
suavemente. ¿Floridos desengaños
dorados por la tarde que declina?
¿Ansias de vida nueva en nuevos años?

　　¿Lamentará la juventud perdida?
Lejos quedó —la pobre loba— muerta.
¿La blanca juventud nunca vivida
teme, que ha de cantar ante su puerta?

　　¿Sonríe al sol de oro,
de la tierra de un sueño no encontrada;
y ve su nave hender el mar sonoro,
de viento y luz la blanca vela henchida?

　　Él ha visto las hojas otoñales,
amarillas, rodar, las olorosas
ramas del eucalipto, los rosales
que enseñan otra vez sus blancas rosas ...

Y este dolor que añora o desconfía
el temblor de una lágrima reprime,
y un resto de viril hipocresía
en el semblante pálido se imprime.

Serio retrato en la pared clarea
todavía. Nosotros divagamos.
En la tristeza del hogar golpea
el tictac del reloj. Todos callamos.

Commentary

The 'viajero' has been identified as the poet's father who returned from Puerto Rico in poor health in February 1893 and died shortly after. This event left the family in straitened finances. Other critics suggest José, Machado's brother, one mentioned in the poem, who also sought a fortune in the Americas. The two figures may be subsumed here into one with the 'viajero' associated with a 'sueño infantil': Machado would be about 10 years old which suggests the father. At the same time, with the reference to the 'serio retrato' on the wall, the 'viajero' may not be there, only his portrait, an absent 'presence'. Alternatively, this 'hermano' may be the poet himself; he refers to himself as 'hermano' as an *alter ego* in poem VI. Thus the poem evokes an 'absence' to suggest the loss the poet confides in this poem; the 'retrato', a Symbolist 'frame', is the poet himself. Real details are wedded to evoked feelings as the 'viajero', present or as portrait, a mirror to Machado's concerns, become the symbolic bearer of them as well as a 'traveller' (a seeker) who, across *SGOP*, will seek to explore these problems. The setting with its further Symbolist frames and spaces –closed room, mirror, picture, window – (see Introduction on Symbolism) form a locus for meditation. Outside passing time is evoked in the fallen leaves, ancient park, etc; inside, the clock and the portrait. The meditation turns from description and evocation to questions of loss: of youth, of dreams, to which the poet responds with stoicism (see poem XCI) and a 'viril hipocresía', a pretence at serenity. Yet the silence of the final lines suggests that the problems remain unresolved, as the following poems show, where Machado repeatedly raises the same questions. For the style of this poem see March-Martul 1982.

Published in *Ateneo*, IV, 1907 and *Renacimiento*, I, March 1907.
Serventesios of 11 syllables with crossed consonantal rhyme.

II

He andado muchos caminos,
he abierto muchas veredas;
he navegado en cien mares,
y atracado en cien riberas.

En todas partes he visto
caravanas de tristeza,
soberbios y melancólicos
borrachos de sombra negra,

y pedantones al paño
que miran, callan, y piensan
que saben, porque no beben
el vino de las tabernas.

Mala gente que camina
y va apestando la tierra ...

Y en todas partes he visto
gentes que danzan o juegan,
cuando pueden, y laboran
sus cuatro palmos de tierra.

Nunca, si llegan a un sitio,
preguntan adonde llegan.
Cuando caminan, cabalgan
a lomos de mula vieja,

y no conocen la prisa
ni aun en los días de fiesta.
Donde hay vino, beben vino;
donde no hay vino, agua fresca.

Son buenas gentes que viven,
laboran, pasan y sueñan,
y en un día como tantos,
descansan bajo la tierra.

Commentary

A contrast of those who live, for Machado and his *institucionista* ideals, an 'authentic' life, the 'buena gente', the humble folk who represent the 'soul' of Spain, and those who do not. For the theme of the 'camino' in Machado see Orozco 1968 and Ruiz Ramón 1962b.

Published in *Renacimiento,* I, March 1907 under the title 'Romance'. Romance in e-a.

III

   La plaza y los naranjos encendidos
con sus frutas redondas y risueñas.

   Tumulto de pequeños colegiales
que, al salir en desorden de la escuela,
llenan el aire de la plaza en sombra
con la algazara de sus voces nuevas.

   ¡Alegría infantil en los rincones
de las ciudades muertas! ...
¡Y algo nuestro de ayer, que todavía
vemos vagar por estas calles viejas!

Commentary

An evocation, with a sigh in the ellipsis in the final stanza, of a timeless continuum, an *intrahistoria* of the 'soul' of Spain suggested in the recall of the everyday sounds of children playing in an ancient town; present and past in one evoked moment. At the same time Machado glimpses something of the past and his own past in these sounds.

Published in *Renacimiento,* I, March 1907 under the title 'Apuntes'. Romance heroico (9 hendecasyllables and 1 heptasyllable) in e-a.

IV

(EN EL ENTIERRO DE UN AMIGO)

Tierra le dieron una tarde horrible
del mes de julio, bajo el sol de fuego.

A un paso de la abierta sepultura,
había rosas de podridos pétalos,
entre geranios de áspera fragancia
y roja flor. El cielo
puro y azul. Corría
un aire fuerte y seco.

De los gruesos cordeles suspendido,
pesadamente, descender hicieron
el ataúd al fondo de la fosa
los dos sepultureros ...

Y al resonar sonó con recio golpe,
solemne, en el silencio.

Un golpe de ataúd en tierra es algo
perfectamente serio.

Sobre la negra caja se rompían
los pesados terrones polvorientos ...

El aire se llevaba
de la honda fosa el blanquecino aliento.

—Y tú, sin sombra ya, duerme y reposa,
larga paz a tus huesos ...

Definitivamente,
duerme un sueño tranquilo y verdadero.

Commentary

Machado starkly evokes the finality of death through symbols of time – heat, fading flowers, scents, wind, the sound of earth on the coffin – and the absence of the dead man's 'sombra' in the penultimate stanza. Yet his thoughts are tempered by his sympathy for his friend who 'dreams' in death, suggesting a continuum rather than an ending. Note the effect of the 'r' and 's' sounds, especially in the fourth stanza.

Published in *Renacimiento*, I, March 1907. Silva-romance (15 hendecasyllables and 9 heptasyllables) in e-o.

V

(RECUERDO INFANTIL)

Una tarde parda y fría
de invierno. Los colegiales
estudian. Monotonía
de lluvia tras los cristales.

Es la clase. En un cartel
se representa a Caín
fugitivo, y muerto Abel,
junto a una mancha carmín.

Con timbre sonoro y hueco
truena el maestro, un anciano
mal vestido, enjuto y seco,
que lleva un libro en la mano.

Y todo un coro infantil
va cantando la lección;
mil veces ciento, cien mil,
mil veces mil, un millón.

Una tarde parda y fría
de invierno. Los colegiales
estudian. Monotonía
de la lluvia en los cristales.

Commentary

Another 'memory' of the monotony of life, here his early childhood schooling evoked through weather, the sounds, the chants, the repetition of the first stanza at the end, the aged and poorly dressed, hence poorly paid, teacher, etc. The repetition of the first and final stanzas also suggests rote learning and want of inspiration, aspects the Institución Libre (where Machado was later taught) strove to change.

Published in *Ateneo*, I, 1906; *Renacimiento*, 1, March 1907. Redondillas with cross rhyme.

VI

Fue una clara tarde, triste y soñolienta ...
tarde de verano. La hiedra asomaba
al muro del parque, negra y polvorienta ...
 La fuente sonaba.

Rechinó en la vieja cancela mi llave;
con agrio ruido abrióse la puerta
de hierro mohoso y, al cerrarse, grave
golpeó el silencio de la tarde muerta.

En el solitario parque, la sonora
copla borbollante del agua cantora
me guía a la fuente. La fuente vertía
sobre el blanco mármol su monotonía.

La fuente cantaba: ¿Te recuerda, hermano,
un sueño lejano mi canto presente?
Fue una tarde lenta del lento verano.

Respondí a la fuente:
No recuerdo, hermana,
mas sé que tu copla presente es lejana.

Fue esta misma tarde: mi cristal vertía
como hoy sobre el mármol su monotonía.
¿Recuerdas, hermano? ... Los mirtos talares,
que ves, sombreaban los claros cantares
que escuchas. Del rubio color de la llama,
el fruto maduro pendía en la rama,
 lo mismo que ahora. ¿Recuerdas, hermano? ...
Fue esta misma lenta tarde de verano.

   　—No sé qué me dice tu copla riente
de ensueños lejanos, hermana la fuente.

   Yo sé que tu claro cristal de alegría
ya supo del árbol la fruta bermeja;
yo sé que es lejana la amargura mía
que sueña en la tarde de verano vieja.

   Yo sé que tus bellos espejos cantores
copiaron antiguos delirios de amores:
mas cuéntame, fuente de lengua encantada,
cuéntame mi alegre leyenda olvidada.

   —Yo no sé leyendas de antigua alegría,
sino historias viejas de melancolía.

   Fue una clara tarde del lento verano ...
Tú venías solo con tu pena, hermano;
tus labios besaron mi linfa serena,
y en la clara tarde, dijeron tu pena.

   Dijeron tu pena tus labios que ardían;
la sed que ahora tienen, entonces tenían.

   —Adiós para siempre la fuente sonora,
del parque dormido eterna cantora.
Adiós para siempre; tu monotonía,
fuente, es más amarga que la pena mía.

   Rechinó en la vieja cancela mi llave;
con agrio ruido abrióse la puerta
de hierro mohoso y, al cerrarse, grave
sonó en el silencio de la tarde muerta.

Commentary

One of Machado's most assured Symbolist poems expressing the issues raised in poem I. The poet enters and leaves a symbolic space (the abandoned garden, a lost paradise) to interrogate himself, the fountain as interlocutor and symbolic Muse associated with the golden fruit on the tree, a symbol of the golden fruit of inspiration from the Woods of Helicon, home of the Muses. See poem XCI and the Appendix. In seeking a lost past and youth of felicity, compared with the sadness of the present – a Romantic contrast – Machado recognises, more poignantly, that he never ever enjoyed any of the things he seeks, exacerbating the then/now contrast of the Romantics. Based loosely on Verlaine's 'Après trois ans' (Machado met Verlaine in Paris in 1899), he employs this Symbolist 'space' as a means of self-analysis. The poem expresses motifs, especially the golden fruit associated with the Muses, which are to recur throughout the collection. See Cardwell 1990; Segre 1970 (two essays on poem VI). For the theme of a lost paradise see Predmore 1974–75 and Oringer 2001.

Mainly dodecasyllable lines with consonantal rhyme.

VII

El limonero lánguido suspende
una pálida rama polvorienta,
sobre el encanto de la fuente limpia,
y allá en el fondo sueñan
los frutos de oro ...

Es una tarde clara,
casi de primavera,
tibia tarde de marzo
que el hálito de abril cercano lleva;
y estoy solo, en el patio silencioso,
buscando una ilusión cándida y vieja:
alguna sombra sobre el blanco muro,
algún recuerdo, en el pretil de piedra
de la fuente dormido, o, en el aire,
algún vagar de túnica ligera.

En el ambiente de la tarde flota
ese aroma de ausencia,
que dice al alma luminosa: nunca,
y al corazón: espera.

Ese aroma que evoca los fantasmas
de las fragancias vírgenes y muertas.

Sí, te recuerdo, tarde alegre y clara,
casi de primavera,
tarde sin flores, cuando me traías
el buen perfume de la hierbabuena,
y de la buena albahaca,
que tenía mi madre en sus macetas.

Que tú me viste hundir mis manos puras
en el agua serena,
para alcanzar los frutos encantados
que hoy en el fondo de la fuente sueñan ...

Sí, te conozco, tarde alegre y clara,
casi de primavera.

Commentary

Another of Machado's most successful poems in exploring the past and his lost childhood illusions. At the same time the poem deals with lost inspiration. Based on a return to the patio of the Palacio de las Dueñas (where he was brought up) in Seville in 1898 or, more probably, 1902, he creates a 'space' in which he probes his earlier illusions to explore, once more, the lost past symbolised in the reflected fruits which 'dream', the shadow, the smells, his mother, etc. But the poem also addresses the nature of inspiration where 'lemons' become symbolic 'frutos de oro', and faces the problem of recalling early pristine emotions and an adequate expression for them. He recalls the moment of loss when the child sought the 'frutos encantados', inspiration of the Muses in the intact mirror, now broken, which remain there but now out of reach, a symbol of lost poetic power which the poem seeks to recall. These are aspects he takes up in other poems, notably XCI. See Cardwell 1990.

Published in *Helios*, I. 1, vii, July 1903 with the title 'El poeta visita el patio de la casa en que nació'. Silva-romance in e-a.

VIII

    Yo escucho los cantos
de viejas cadencias,
que los niños cantan
cuando en coro juegan
y vierten en coro
sus almas que sueñan,
cual vierten sus aguas
las fuentes de piedra;
con monotonías
de risas eternas,
que no son alegres,
con lágrimas viejas,
que no son amargas
y dicen tristezas,
tristezas de amores
de antiguas leyendas.

    En los labios niños,
las canciones llevan
confusa la historia
y clara la pena;
como clara el agua
lleva su conseja
de viejos amores,
que nunca se cuentan.

    Jugando, a la sombra
de una plaza vieja,
los niños cantaban ...

    La fuente de piedra
vertía su eterno
cristal de leyenda.

    Cantaban los niños
canciones ingenuas,
de un algo que pasa

y que nunca llega:
la historia confusa
y clara la pena.

   Seguía su cuento
la fuente serena;
borrada la historia,
contaba la pena.

Commentary

A reprise of poem III where children's songs and dreams, in parallel with the flow of fountains (time passing), are used to create a timeless present. The 'soul' of Spain is expressed in popular verse – 'viejas cadencias' – intertwined with an unspoken personal sadness as if something has been lost. The songs and the children's 'dreams' create a screen onto which the poet projects his thoughts and the sense of what he has lost and what cannot be recovered. Thus timeless present and time passing are contrasted, a dilemma Machado will never resolve. See Ribbans, 1971, 171–2.

   Hexasyllabic *romancillo* in e–a.

IX

(ORILLAS DEL DUERO).

   Se ha asomado una cigüeña a lo alto del campanario.
Girando en torno a la torre y al caserón solitario,
y las golondrinas chillan. Pasaron del blanco invierno,
de nevascas y ventiscas los crudos soplos de infierno.
Es una tibia mañana.
El sol calienta un poquito la pobre tierra soriana.

   Pasados los verdes pinos,
casi azules, primavera
se ve brotar en los finos
chopos de la carretera
y del río. El Duero corre, terso y mudo, mansamente.
El campo parece, más que joven, adolescente.

Entre las hierbas alguna humilde flor ha nacido,
azul o blanca. ¡Belleza del campo apenas florido,
y mística primavera!

¡Chopos del camino blanco, álamos de la ribera,
espuma de la montaña
ante la azul lejanía
sol del día, claro día!
¡Hermosa tierra de España!

Commentary

In early May 1907 Machado first went to Soria to take up a teaching post in the local Instituto. Probably the first Soria poem. Note the realism of the description, anticipating *Campos de Castilla* of 1912, presenting a new contact with nature. The attention to natural elements comes from his education and the nature walks taken by the Institución Libre in the late 1880s. This new vision of nature is repeated in many poems in *SGOP*.

A combination of decahexasyllables and octosyllables in couplets or in alternate rhyme. Compare with XIII and XVIII.

X

A la desierta plaza
conduce un laberinto de callejas.
A un lado, el viejo paredón sombrío
de una ruinosa iglesia;
a otro lado, la tapia blanquecina
de un huerto de cipreses y palmeras,
y, frente a mí, la casa,
y en la casa la reja
ante el cristal que levemente empaña
su figurilla plácida y risueña.
Me apartaré. No quiero
llamar a tu ventana ... Primavera
viene —su veste blanca

flota en el aire de la plaza muerta—;
viene a encender las rosas
rojas de tus rosales ... Quiero verla ...

Commentary

The evocation of this ancient, crumbling town is in tune with the search for the 'soul' of Spain and the work of his contemporaries, notably his friend, Azorín and contemporary painters: Zuloaga, Vázquez Díaz, Solana. But the poem also hints at an impossible love encounter (inspired by Bécquer's 'Tres fechas'?) symbolising something that has been lost. *Helios,* I, I, vii, July 1903 with the title 'El poeta encuentra esta nota en su carta'.

Silva-romance in e-a (hendecasyllables and 7 heptasyllables).

XI

Yo voy soñando caminos
de la tarde. ¡Las colinas
doradas, los verdes pinos,
las polvorientas encinas! ...
¿Adonde el camino irá?
Yo voy cantando, viajero
a lo largo del sendero ...
—La tarde cayendo está—,
'En el corazón tenía
la espina de una pasión;
logré arrancármela un día:
ya no siento el corazón.'

Y todo el campo un momento
se queda, mudo y sombrío,
meditando. Suena el viento
en los álamos del río.
La tarde más se obscurece;
y el camino que serpea
y débilmente blanquea,
se enturbia y desaparece.

Mi cantar vuelve a plañir:
'Aguda espina dorada,
quién te pudiera sentir
en el corazón clavada.'

Commentary

The landscape is used as a screen for a personal meditation. But this is overlaid with glosses of the Sevillian *saeta* (a lament recalling the symbolic arrows in the breast of the Virgin Mary at Christ's death and sung in the Easter processions), fused with a song of love's rejection. It is the poet, not the 'campo' who meditates – a trope of Symbolism, the *paysage d'âme* – and the darkening landscape suggest lost illusions and forlorn hopes, thoughts reinforced by the final *saeta*. The poem fuses personal concerns and an evocation of the 'soul' of Andalucía as well as glossing San Juan de la Cruz, Santa Teresa and Rosalía de Castro. See Ferreres 1964.

Published in *Ateneo*, I, 1906, entitled 'Ensueños'. Redondillas with cross rhyme.

XII

Amada, el aura dice
tu pura veste blanca ...
No te verán mis ojos
¡mi corazón te aguarda!

El viento me ha traído
tu nombre en la mañana;
el eco de tus pasos
repite la montaña ...
No te verán, mis ojos;
¡mi corazón te aguarda!

En las sombrías torres
repican las campanas ...
No te verán mis ojos;
¡mi corazón te aguarda!

    Los golpes del martillo
dicen la negra caja;
y el sitio de la fosa,
los golpes de la azada ...
No te verán mis ojos;
¡mi corazón te aguarda!

Commentary

Machado suggests the death of the *amada* (or of inspiration?) yet the hope of a reunion. Yet this is a symbolic statement in that the time markers – aura, viento, campanas – suggest, too, the death of a longed for ideal.

Heptasyllabic romance in a-a.

XIII

    Hacia un ocaso radiante
caminaba el sol de estío,
y era, entre nubes de fuego, una trompeta gigante,
tras de los álamos verdes de las márgenes del río.

    Dentro de un olmo sonaba la sempiterna tijera
de la cigarra cantora, el monorritmo jovial,
entre metal y madera,
que es la canción estival.

    En una huerta sombría,
giraban los cangilones de la noria soñolienta.
Bajo las ramas obscuras el son del agua se oía.
Era una tarde de julio, luminosa y polvorienta.

    Yo iba haciendo mi camino,
absorto en el solitario crepúsculo campesino.

    Y pensaba: '¡Hermosa tarde, nota de la lira inmensa
toda desdén y armonía;
hermosa tarde, tú curas la pobre melancolía
de este rincón vanidoso, obscuro rincón que piensa!'

Pasaba el agua rizada bajo los ojos del puente.
Lejos la ciudad dormía,
como cubierta de un mago fanal de oro transparente.
Bajo los arcos de piedra el agua clara corría.

  Los últimos arreboles coronaban las colinas
manchadas de olivos grises y de negruzcas encinas.
Yo caminaba cansado,
sintiendo la vieja angustia que hace el corazón pesado.

  El agua en sombra pasaba tan melancólicamente,
bajo los arcos del puente,
como si al pasar dijera:

  'Apenas desamarrada
la pobre barca, viajero, del árbol de la ribera,
se canta: no somos nada.
Donde acaba el pobre río la inmensa mar nos espera.'

  Bajo los ojos del puente pasaba el agua sombría.
(Yo pensaba: ¡el alma mía!)

  Y me detuve un momento,
en la tarde, a meditar ...
¿Qué es esta gota en el viento
que grita al mar: soy el mar?

  Vibraba el aire asordado
por los élitros cantores que hacen el campo sonoro,
cual si estuviera sembrado
de campanitas de oro.

  En el azul fulguraba
un lucero diamantino.
Cálido viento soplaba,
alborotando el camino.

  Yo, en la tarde polvorienta,
hacia la ciudad volvía.
Sonaban los cangilones de la noria soñolienta.
Bajo las ramas obscuras caer el agua se oía.

Commentary

Probably a late poem set in the Sorian landscape. But the stroll through this new countryside becomes a symbol and meditation on passing time and the poet's 'pobre melancolía' and 'vieja angustia'. He overlays emotions on natural elements – 'El agua ... pasaba ... melancólicamente' –, he glosses a popular song and meditates on time's flux: his return, the 'noria' and flowing water. Based on a poly-rhythymic hexadecasyllable structure with quartets of octosyllables and other variants. Possibly experimental in line with the early phase of Spanish Symbolism.

Published in *Los Lunes de El Imparcial*, 22-IX-1906 with the title 'Soledades'. Poly-rhythmic hendecasyllables with 8s and 16s.

XIV

(CANTE HONDO)

Yo meditaba absorto, devanando
los hilos del hastío y la tristeza,
cuando llegó a mi oído,
por la ventana de mi estancia, abierta

a una caliente noche de verano,
el plañir de una copla soñolienta,
quebrada por los trémolos sombríos
de las músicas magas de mi tierra.

... Y era el Amor, como una roja llama.
—Nerviosa mano en la vibrante cuerda
ponía un largo suspirar de oro,
que se trocaba en surtidor de estrellas—.

... Y era la Muerte, al hombro la cuchilla,
el paso largo, torva y esquelética,
—tal cuando yo era niño la soñaba—.

Y en la guitarra, resonante y trémula,
la brusca mano, al golpear, fingía
el reposar de un ataúd en tierra.

Y era un plañido solitario el soplo
que el polvo barre y la ceniza avienta.

Commentary

Machado was an *aficionado* of *cante hondo* in the Seville of his youth. The poem expresses inner sadness and thoughts of death, as does the traditional *cante* which almost always expresses doomed love and death. The music reminds the poet of his homeland (timeless Spain again) but the poem ends on the motif of 'dust to dust ...'.

Published in *Los Lunes de El Imparcial*, 28-I-1907 with poem XXXIX with the title 'Soledades'. Romance heroico in e-a in hendecasyllables and 1 heptasyllable.

XV

La calle en sombra. Ocultan los altos caserones
el sol que muere; hay ecos de luz en los balcones.

¿No ves, en el encanto del mirador florido,
óvalo rosado de un rostro conocido?

La imagen, tras el vidrio de equívoco reflejo,
surge o se apaga como daguerrotipo viejo.

Suena en la calle sólo el ruido de tu paso;
se extinguen lentamente los ecos del ocaso.

¡Oh, angustia! Pesa y duele el corazón ... ¿Es ella?
No puede ser ... Camina ... En el azul, la estrella.

Commentary

A poem linked to poem X with an added emphasis on the fleeting figure in the window, symbol of lost love and failed illusions.

Published in *Renacimiento,* I, March 1907, entitled 'En sueños'. Alexandrines.

XVI

Siempre fugitiva y siempre
cerca de mí, en negro manto
mal cubierto el desdeñoso
gesto de tu rostro pálido.
No sé adonde vas, ni dónde
tu virgen belleza tálamo
busca en la noche. No sé
qué sueños cierran tus párpados,
ni de quién haya entreabierto
tu lecho inhospitalario.

*   *   *

Detén el paso, belleza
esquiva, detén el paso.

Besar quisiera la amarga,
amarga flor de tus labios.

Commentary

One of a group of poems which include elements of the Symbolist Decadence. He evokes a death-like mysterious female figure, the finisecular *femme fatale/* deadly flower who destroys, symbol, too, of a prohibited beauty and a revelation that brings sadness. Note the repeated 'amarga'.
'Noche' in the *Soledades* (1903). Romance in a-o.

XVII

(HORIZONTE)

En una tarde clara y amplia como el hastío,
cuando su lanza blande el tórrido verano,
copiaban el fantasma de un grave sueño mío
mil sombras en teoría, enhiestas, sobre el llano.

La gloria del ocaso era un purpúreo espejo,
era un cristal de llamas, que al infinito viejo
iba, arrojando el grave soñar en la llanura ...
Y yo sentí la espuela sonora de mi paso
repercutir lejana en el sangriento ocaso,
y más allá, la alegre canción de un alba pura.

Commentary

A Symbolist overlay of mood and a meditation on a natural scene. Beginning with similes for his 'grave sueño mío', the sunset becomes a mirror to a lost past, an 'infinito viejo', casting dreams aside. But beyond the blood-red setting sun (pain and distress) lies the hint of happiness cast in religious terms, 'un alba pura', a time (and place) always beyond reach.

   Serventesios with a *décima* of alexandrines.

XVIII

(EL POETA)

Para el libro *La casa de la primavera* de Gregorio Martínez Sierra

   Maldiciendo su destino
como Glauco, el dios marino,
mira, turbia la pupila
de llanto, el mar, que le debe su blanca virgen Scyla.

   El sabe que un Dios más fuerte
con la sustancia inmortal está jugando a la muerte,
cual niño bárbaro. Él piensa
que ha de caer como rama que sobre las aguas flota,
antes de perderse, gota
de mar en la mar inmensa.

   En sueños oyó el acento de una palabra divina;
en sueños se le ha mostrado la cruda ley diamantina,
sin odio ni amor, y el frío
soplo del olvido sabe, sobre un arenal de hastío.

Bajo las palmeras del oasis el agua buena
miró brotar de la arena;
y se abrevó entre las dulces gacelas, y entre los fieros
animales carniceros ...

   Y supo cuánto es la vida hecha de sed y de dolor.
Y fue compasivo para el ciervo y el cazador,
para el ladrón y el robado,
para el pájaro azorado,
para el sanguinario azor.

   Con el sabio amargo dijo: Vanidad de vanidades,
todo es negra vanidad;
y oyó otra voz que clamaba, alma de sus soledades:
sólo eres tú, luz que fulges en el corazón, verdad.

   Y viendo cómo lucían
miles de blancas estrellas,
pensaba que todas ellas
en su corazón ardían.
¡Noche de amor!

   Y otra noche
sintió la mala tristeza
que enturbia la pura llama,
y el corazón que bosteza,
y el histrión que declama.

   Y dijo: Las galerías
del alma que espera están
desiertas, mudas, vacías:
las blancas sombras se van.

   Y el demonio de los sueños abrió el jardín encantado
del ayer. ¡Cuan bello era!
¡Qué hermosamente el pasado
fingía la primavera,
cuando del árbol de otoño estaba el fruto colgado,
mísero fruto podrido,
que en el hueco acibarado
guarda el gusano escondido!

¡Alma, que en vano quisiste ser más joven cada día,
arranca tu flor, la humilde flor de la melancolía!

Commentary

Dedicated to his *Helios* friend, Martínez Sierra, author of fairy tales, stories and Symbolist dramas. The poem was dedicated to Martínez Sierra's book along with poems by Darío and Jiménez. The garden motif Machado employs here and *passim* in *SGOP* echoes Santiago Rusiñol's *Jardines de España* published by Martínez Sierra, a token of the closenesss of the *Helios* circle. At the same time the garden is a Symbolist trope. Machado glosses a myth from Ovid's *Metamorphoses*, Book XIII, to create a poem of meditation and self-interrogation. With additional echoes of Ronsard, the French medieval poet, and the creation of an alter ego (one of many which Machado is to create later in life) the poem relates his preoccupation with failing poetic powers and ebbing inspiration which is symbolised by the references to the sacred springs of Hippocrene and Helicon associated with the Muses (see poems VI and XCI and the Appendix) The dream is cast as poetic knowledge swaying between despair and exultation, a poetic *via negativa*. The final section of the poem addresses a theme which is to reappear: the frustrated promise of poetic inspiration, where the poet sees himself as a 'histrión' playing an inauthentic part cast on a stage which is empty and bereft of illumination. Even when his demon-muse opens the 'jardín encantado', the promised golden fruit, symbol of poetic inspiration, has a worm in its heart. Yet he must set his 'melancolía' aside and strive onwards. An experimental rhyme scheme with measures of 16, 8, redondillas, etc., typical of the revolutionary measures of Latin American poets and Jiménez's and Villaespesa's collections of 1900. See Ribbans, 1971, 221–5. See also Cardwell 1992 and the detailed analysis of this poem by Xon Ros 2010. For Machado's 'galerías' see Palley 1975 and Mattauch 2003 who traces the 'galería' motif to Joris-Karl Huymans' *À Rebours* which Machado may have read in Paris in 1899.

XIX

¡Verdes jardinillos,
claras plazoletas,
fuente verdinosa
donde el agua sueña,
donde el agua muda
resbala en la piedra! ...

Las hojas de un verde
mustio, casi negras
de la acacia, el viento
de septiembre besa,
y se lleva algunas
amarillas, secas,
jugando, entre el polvo
blanco de la tierra.

Linda doncellita,
que el cántaro llenas
de agua transparente,
tú, al verme, no llevas
a los negros bucles
de tu cabellera,
distraídamente,
la mano morena,
ni, luego, en el limpio
cristal te contemplas ...

Tú miras al aire
de la tarde bella,
mientras de agua clara
el cántaro llenas.

Commentary

Machado evokes another Symbolist 'space', again a closed garden with a fountain in autumn, a marker of passing time. The girl at the well, symbol once more of a timeless present, and the 'soul' of Spain, who, unlike the poet who meditates on time and passing time, looks to the heavens as she collects the 'pure' water.

Hexasyllabic romancillo in e-a.

Del camino

XX

(PRELUDIO)

    Mientras la sombra pasa de un santo amor, hoy quiero
poner un dulce salmo sobre mi viejo atril.
Acordaré las notas del órgano severo
al suspirar fragante del pífano de abril.

    Madurarán su aroma las pomas otoñales,
la mirra y el incienso salmodiarán su olor;
exhalarán su fresco perfume los rosales,
bajo la paz en sombra del tibio huerto en flor.

    Al grave acorde lento de música y aroma,
la sola y vieja y noble razón de mi rezar
levantará su vuelo suave de paloma,
y la palabra blanca se elevará al altar.

Commentary

The religious and sensual evocations in this early poem suggest, again, the presence of Decadent Symbolism. Through sacred images –salmo, órgano, mirra, incienso, etc. – and sensual smells, the poem seeks to express an aesthetic ideal, the ultimate 'Word', 'la palabra blanca', here expressed in the symbolic dove of the Holy Spirit. The Decadence frequently employed religious terms for aesthetic ones. The poem is a 'hymn' to lost illusions, the 'sombra ... de un santo amor'.

    Alexandrine serventesios with rhyme in paired lines.

XXI

Daba el reloj las doce ... y eran doce
golpes de azada en tierra ...
...¡Mi hora! —grité—. ... El silencio
me respondió: —No temas;
tú no verás caer la última gota
que en la clepsidra tiembla.

Dormirás muchas horas todavía
sobre la orilla vieja,
y encontrarás una mañana pura
amarrada tu barca a otra ribera.

Commentary

Another meditation on mortality and the sought-for reassurance that his words might transcend death and time.

Published in *Revista Ibérica*, 3, 20-VIII-1902 with the title 'Del camino' with alterations in SGOP, and in *Los Lunes de El Imparcial*, 16-VII-1907. Silva romance in e-a.

XXII

Sobre la tierra amarga,
caminos tiene el sueño
laberínticos, sendas tortuosas,
parques en flor y en sombra y en silencio

criptas hondas, escalas sobre estrellas;
retablos de esperanzas y recuerdos.
Figurillas que pasan y sonríen
—juguetes melancólicos de viejo—;

imágenes amigas,
a la vuelta florida del sendero,
y quimeras rosadas
que hacen camino ... lejos ...

Commentary

One of a series of poems which evoke the difficulties of expressing the world of dream and inspiration, a major Symbolist preoccupation. Following on from the end of poem XVIII, Machado evokes a series of terms for the confusing pathways to a possible illumination: the recurrent image of the 'camino', the 'laberinto', 'senda', 'escala', etc., which turn, as before, into theatrical images. Thus while the poet is lost in a maze of paths, at the same time he queries whether his search is mere play-acting, insincere, inauthentic or not? Again there are hints of the Decadence in the fleeting figures which invite the poet to an uncertain goal. See also poem XXX.

Silva romance in e-o.

XXIII

En la desnuda tierra del camino
la hora florida brota,
espino solitario,
del valle humilde en la revuelta umbrosa.

El salmo verdadero
de tenue voz hoy torna
al corazón, y al labio,
la palabra quebrada y temblorosa.

Mis viejos mares duermen; se apagaron
sus espumas sonoras
sobre la playa estéril. La tormenta
camina lejos en la nube torva.

Vuelve la paz al cielo;
la brisa tutelar esparce aromas
otra vez sobre el campo, y aparece,
en la bendita soledad, tu sombra.

Commentary

With echoes of the Psalms and the Old Testament, Machado 'hears' the 'Word' he seeks but it is 'quebrada y temblorosa'. The symbolic sea of thought, like the beach, is 'estéril'. With an echo of the return of the dove to the Ark as the storm moves away, Machado glimpses the lost 'sombra' in 'la bendita soledad', symbol of the ultimate 'Word' he seeks.

Published in *Los Lunes de El Imparcial*, 16-VII-1906 under the title 'Del camino'. Silva romance in o-a.

XXIV

El sol es un globo de fuego,
la luna es un disco morado.

Una blanca paloma se posa
en el alto ciprés centenario.

Los cuadros de mirtos parecen
de marchito velludo empolvado.

¡El jardín y la tarde tranquila! ...
Suena el agua en la fuente de mármol.

Commentary

A series of natural elements, possibly based on a Sevillian garden, suggest a timeless moment which is threatened by the flow of water at the end, symbol of the erosion of time. There is a hint of Decadent artifice in the first stanza and the evocation of the myrtles, associated in tradition with the God of Poetry, Apollo.

Silva romance in a-o.

XXV

¡Tenue rumor de túnicas que pasan
sobre la infértil tierra! ...

¡Y lágrimas sonoras
de las campanas viejas!

Las ascuas mortecinas
del horizonte humean ...
Blancos fantasmas lares
van encendiendo estrellas.

—Abre el balcón. La hora
De una ilusión se acerca ...
La tarde se ha dormido,
y las campanas sueñan.

Commentary

Machado evokes here, as elsewhere, figures in a Greek Doric dress, a *chiton*, possibly the Muses whom he portrays elsewhere, notably in poem XCI, here in terms of infertility and the 'tears' of bells (overlay of emotion in a *paysage d'âme*). As the sun sets he notes a change and with the opening of the balcony he senses the 'ilusión' he seeks as the bells, like the poet, 'dream'. See Cardwell 1992.

Published in *Revista Ibérica*, 3, 20-VIII-1902 under the title 'Del camino', subsequently revised in *SGOP*. Silva romance in a-o.

XXVI

¡Oh, figuras del atrio, más humildes
cada día y lejanas:
mendigos harapientos
sobre marmóreas gradas;

miserables ungidos
de eternidades santas,

manos que surgen de los mantos viejos
y de las rotas capas!

   ¿Pasó por vuestro lado
una ilusión velada,
de la mañana luminosa y fría
en las horas más plácidas? ...

   Sobre la negra túnica, su mano
era una rosa blanca ...

Commentary

Through the beggars, who daily sit at the church door, Machado creates a timeless continuum, an *intrahistoria*, witness to his lost and past illusions. But does the 'mano' belong to the beggar or is it, again, the Decadent female, bearer of the lost world of the 'ilusión velada'? Or are the beggars a symbol of the poet himself who seeks to recall 'una ilusión velada ... en horas más plácidas'?

   Published in *Revista Ibérica*, 20-VIII-1902 under the title 'Del camino', revised in *SGOP*. Silva romance in a-a.

XXVII

   La tarde todavía
dará incienso de oro a tu plegaria,
y quizás el cenit de un nuevo día
amenguará tu sombra solitaria.

Mas no es tu fiesta el ultramar lejano,
sino la ermita junto al manso río;
no tu sandalia el soñoliento llano
pisará, ni la arena del hastío.

   Muy cerca está, romero,
la tierra verde y santa y florecida
de tus sueños; muy cerca, peregrino
que desdeñas la sombra del sendero
y el agua del mesón en tu camino.

Commentary

The poet creates an alter ego as a 'tú' as he contemplates a golden sunset and aspires to a new dawn with the hope of breaking his solitude. Yet, he admits, he is alone. He senses, despite his solitude and rejection, even frustration, that the ideal is near. Note the religious terms in an aesthetic meditation (Decadence again): 'incienso', 'plegaria, 'ermita, and the insistence on his search as a pilgrimage: 'romero', 'peregrino'. Again the overlay of religion on aesthetic concerns in the desired poetic 'tierra verde y santa' in an echo of the Psalms. For this theme of frustration/desire see Reyrègne 2000.

Published in *Revista Ibérica*, 3, 20-VIII-1902 under the title 'Del camino' revised in *SGOP*. Silva in 11 and 7 syllables.

XXVIII

Crear fiestas de amores
en nuestro amor pensamos,
quemar nuevos aromas
en montes no pisados,

y guardar el secreto
de nuestros rostros pálidos,
porque en las bacanales de la vida
vacías nuestras copas conservamos,

mientras con eco de cristal y espuma
ríen los zumos de la vid dorados.

Un pájaro escondido entre las ramas
del parque solitario,
silba burlón ...

Nosotros exprimimos
la penumbra de un sueño en nuestro vaso ...
Y algo, que es tierra en nuestra carne, siente
la humedad del jardín como un halago.

Commentary

A gloss of the verses of Anacreon (a Greek poet of c.530 BC), popular in the *fin de siglo*, especially in the Decadence and in the poetry of his friend, Rubén Darío, which Machado knew. He re-uses the theme of revelry to suggest a contrastive 'vacías copas' with the desire for 'vid dorados', a reprise of the golden fruit of the Muses. The image of the trodden grape is recast as the sensed dream ('penumbra') of a new space, the Symbolist garden where the birdsong mocks.

Published in *Los Lunes de El Imparcial*, 16-VII-1906 under the title 'Del camino'. Silva romance in a-o.

XXIX

Arde en tus ojos un misterio, virgen
esquiva y compañera.

No sé si es odio o es amor la lumbre
inagotable de tu aljaba negra.

Conmigo irás mientras proyecte sombra
mi cuerpo y quede a mi sandalia arena.

—¿Eres la sed o el agua en mi camino?
Dime, virgen esquiva y compañera.

Commentary

Once more the evocation of a Decadent *femme fatale*, the dangerous muse who both tempts and fulfils. See also XVI and XXV.
Silva romance in e-a.

XXX

    Algunos lienzos del recuerdo tienen
luz de jardín y soledad de campo
la placidez del sueño
en el paisaje familiar soñado.

    Otros guardan las fiestas
de días aun lejanos;
figurillas sutiles
que pone un titerero en su retablo ...

Ante el balcón florido,
está la cita de un amor amargo.

    Brilla la tarde en el resol bermejo ...
La hiedra efunde de los muros blancos ...

  A la revuelta de una calle en sombra,
un fantasma irrisorio besa un nardo.

Commentary

The recall of memory is cast in terms of spaces and frames: 'lienzo', 'jardín', 'paisaje'. Some are positive while others seem to mock as shadows on a stage (see XXII). But memories are of failed love amid a sense of passing time, sunset, ivy and the image of the *femme fatale* bearing a Decadent flower, the spikenard (tuberose).
    Published in *Revista Ibérica*, 3, 20-VIII-1902 under the title 'Del camino' and revised in *SGOP*. Silva romance in a-o.

XXXI

    Crece en la plaza en sombra
el musgo, y en la piedra vieja y santa
de la iglesia. En el atrio hay un mendigo ..
Más vieja que la iglesia tiene el alma.

Sube muy lento, en las mañanas frías,
por la marmórea grada,
hasta un rincón de piedra ... Allí aparece
su mano seca entre la rota capa.

   Con las órbitas huecas de sus ojos
ha visto cómo pasan
las blancas sombras, en los claros días,
las blancas sombras de las horas santas.

Commentary

Through images of passing time ('sombra', 'musgo') Machado evokes, in the beggar, a timeless present figuring the 'soul' of Spain, witness to the continuum of time (see XXVI). At the same time the beggar is a symbol of the poet himself, he has also witnessed 'las blancas sombras', symbols of a past felicity now gone.

Published in *Revista Ibérica*, 3, 20-VIII-1902 under the title 'Del camino' and revised in SGOP. Silva romance in 9 and 7.

XXXII

   Las ascuas de un crepúsculo morado
detrás del negro cipresal humean ...
En la glorieta en sombra está la fuente
con su alado y desnudo Amor de piedra,
que sueña mudo. En la marmórea taza
reposa el agua muerta.

Commentary

Note the emphasis on funereal colours and the overlay of the poet's mood on the evoked scene with a possible echo of Mallarmé's 'Les Fenêtres'. It is the poet who dreams, of course, not the statue. Here Love is mute, inert in stone. Again he creates the sense of loss and time's erosion in 'agua muerta'. See Bousoño 1952, Ferreres 1964 and Ribbans 1971.

   Silva romance in 11 and 7.

XXXIII

¿Mi amor?... ¿Recuerdas, dime,
aquellos juncos tiernos,
lánguidos y amarillos
que hay en el cauce seco?...

¿Recuerdas la amapola
que calcinó el verano,
la amapola marchita,
negro crespón del campo?...

¿Te acuerdas del sol yerto
y humilde, en la mañana,
que brilla y tiembla roto
sobre una fuente helada?...

Commentary

One of many poems where Machado creates a dialogue with an inanimate object (see VI, for example). Here the poet enquires of a past love to which he responds negatively through a series of Decadent Symbolist images: dying reeds, shrivelled poppy, dying sun, frozen fountain all suggesting that the summer of love is gone.
Couplets of 7.

XXXIV

Me dijo un alba de la primavera:
Yo florecí en tu corazón sombrío
ha muchos años, caminante viejo
que no cortas las flores del camino.

Tu corazón de sombra, ¿acaso guarda
el viejo aroma de mis viejos lirios?
¿Perfuman aún mis rosas la alba frente
del hada de tu sueño adamantino?

Respondí a la mañana:
Sólo tienen cristal los sueños míos.
Yo no conozco el hada de mis sueños;
ni sé si está mi corazón florido.

Pero si aguardas la mañana pura
que ha de romper el vaso cristalino,
quizás el hada te dará tus rosas,
mi corazón tus lirios.

Commentary

The poet's dreams are portrayed here, as elsewhere, in Symbolist terms of reflecting glass and absences. Yet he longs for the moment when the 'vaso cristalino' (the empty glass of poem XXVIII?) will break and his imagination will flower, a process depicted in Decadent terms, the muse offering him roses and irises (love and death).

XXXV

Al borde del sendero un día nos sentamos.
Ya nuestra vida es tiempo, y nuestra sola cuita
son las desesperantes posturas que tomamos
para aguardar ... Mas Ella no faltará a la cita.

Commentary

A meditation on inevitable death and passing time stressing the various strategies taken to avoid thoughts of one's own finality.
Alexandrine serventesios.

XXXVI

Es una forma juvenil que un día
a nuestra casa llega.
Nosotros le decimos: ¿por qué tornas
a la morada vieja?
Ella abre la ventana, y todo el campo
en luz y aroma entra.
En el blanco sendero,
los troncos de los árboles negrean;
las hojas de sus copas
son humo verde que a lo lejos sueña.
Parece una laguna
el ancho río entre la blanca niebla
de la mañana. Por los montes cárdenos
camina otra quimera.

Commentary

Once more the phantom female figure – a muse? – and the colloquy between her and the poet. Again a glowing and sensual landscape in bright, typically Decadent colours, but based on known realities, possibly Soria, here used as a moodscape. The poet 'dreams' not the leaves. In the far distance, and out of touch, lies a possible union with the goal he seeks.

Silva romance in 11 and 7.

XXXVII

¡Oh, dime, noche amiga, amada vieja,
que me traes el retablo de mis sueños
siempre desierto y desolado, y sólo
con mi fantasma dentro,
mi pobre sombra triste
sobre la estepa y bajo el sol de fuego,
o soñando amarguras

en las voces de todos los misterios,
dime, si sabes, vieja amada, dime
si son mías las lágrimas que vierto!
Me respondió la noche:
Jamás me revelaste tu secreto.
Yo nunca supe, amado,
si eras tú ese fantasma de tu sueño,
ni averigüé si era su voz la tuya,
o era la voz de un histrión grotesco.

    Dije a la noche: Amada mentirosa,
tú sabes mi secreto;
tú has visto la honda gruta
donde fabrica su cristal mi sueño,
y sabes que mis lágrimas son mías.
y sabes mi dolor, mi dolor viejo.

    ¡Oh! Yo no sé, dijo la noche, amado,
yo no sé tu secreto,
aunque he visto vagar ese que dices
desolado fantasma, por tu sueño.
Yo me asomo a las almas cuando lloran
y escucho su hondo rezo,
humilde y solitario,
ese que llamas salmo verdadero;
pero en las hondas bóvedas del alma
no sé si el llanto es una voz o un eco.

    Para escuchar tu queja de tus labios
yo te busqué en tu sueño,
y allí te vi vagando en un borroso
laberinto de espejos.

Commentary

A further exploration of the role of the poet (see VII) and the nature of inspiration. The process is shadowed forth in another mono-dialogue, here with the night. Once more the use of symbolic spaces and frames – 'retablo', 'gruta', 'bóveda', 'laberinto' (see XVII, XXII and XXX) – to explore the sources and nature of his inspiration and the goal of his search. Can there be a sincere voice? Or is it all a mirage? Note the symbolic use of images of glass, mirrors and religious terms to express his poetic doubts.

Published in *Ateneo*, IV, 1907. Silva romance in e-o.

Canciones

XXXVIII

    Abril florecía
frente a mi ventana.
Entre los jazmines
y las rosas blancas
de un balcón florido,
vi las dos hermanas.
La menor cosía,
la mayor hilaba ...
Entre los jazmines
y las rosas blancas,
la más pequeñita,
risueña y rosada
—su aguja en el aire—,
miró a mi ventana.

    La mayor seguía,
silenciosa y pálida,
el huso en su rueca
que el lino enroscaba.
Abril florecía
frente a mi ventana.

    Una clara tarde
la mayor lloraba,
entre los jazmines
y las rosas blancas,
y ante el blanco lino
que en su rueca hilaba.
— ¿Qué tienes? —le dije—,
silenciosa y pálida,
señaló el vestido
que empezó la hermana.
En la negra túnica
la aguja brillaba;

sobre el blanco velo,
el dedal de plata.
Señaló a la tarde
de abril que soñaba,
mientras que se oía
tañer de campanas.
Y en la clara tarde
me enseñó sus lágrimas ...
Abril florecía
frente a mi ventana.

    Fue otro abril alegre
y otra tarde plácida.
El balcón florido
solitario estaba ...
Ni la pequeñita
risueña y rosada,
ni la hermana triste,
silenciosa y pálida,
ni la negra túnica,
ni la toca blanca ...
Tan sólo en el huso
el lino giraba
por mano invisible,
y en la obscura sala
la luna del limpio
espejo brillaba ...
Entre los jazmines
y las rosas blancas
del balcón florido,
me miré en la clara
luna del espejo
que lejos soñaba ...
Abril florecía
frente a mi ventana.

Commentary

Like his contemporaries, especially Azorín, Machado evokes a traditional scene taken from popular song and stories, a timeless moment of the 'soul' of Spain. The poem was entitled 'Canciones' in *Soledades*. At the same time he suggests the presence of time and death through the image of the loom associated with the three Fates. Note, too, the contrast of flowing spring, the still loom and empty mirror.

Romancillo in 6s in a-a.

XXXIX

(COPLAS ELEGIACAS)

¡Ay del que llega sediento
a ver el agua correr,
y dice: la sed que siento
no me la calma el beber!

¡Ay de quien bebe y, saciada
la sed, desprecia la vida:
moneda al tahur prestada,
que sea al azar rendida!

Del iluso que suspira
bajo el orden soberano,
y del que sueña la lira
pitagórica en su mano.

¡Ay del noble peregrino
que se para a meditar,
después de largo camino
en el horror de llegar!

¡Ay de la melancolía
que llorando se consuela,
y de la melomanía
de un corazón de zarzuela!

¡Ay de nuestro ruiseñor,
si en una noche serena
se cura del mal de amor
que llora y canta sin pena!

¡De los jardines secretos,
de los pensiles soñados,
y de los sueños poblados
de propósitos discretos!

¡Ay del galán sin fortuna
que ronda a la luna bella;
de cuantos caen de la luna,
de cuantos se marchan a ella!

¡De quien el fruto prendido
en la rama no alcanzó,
de quien el fruto ha mordido
y el gusto amargo probó!

¡Y de nuestro amor primero
y de su fe mal pagada,
y, también, del verdadero
amante de nuestra amada!

Commentary

A gloss on a popular *copla,* used to express, in a semi-humouristic way, his own sense of loss and failure as a poet (see ll. 11–12). He casts himself in a series of classic roles of those who fail or cannot complete their desires: the thirsty man who fails to drink, the gambler, the 'iluso poeta', himself, the pilgrim who fears to end his journey, the singer in a popular opera, the failed dreamer, the would-be lover, the disappointed gatherer of fruit.

Published in *Los Lunes de El Imparcial,* 28-I-1907 under the title 'Soledades'. Originally entitled 'De la vida' (*Coplas elegíacas*). Cross rhymed redondillas.

XL

(INVENTARIO GALANTE)

    Tus ojos me recuerdan
las noches de verano,
negras noches sin luna,
orilla al mar salado,
y el chispear de estrellas
del cielo negro y bajo.
Tus ojos me recuerdan.
las noches de verano.
Y tu morena carne,
los trigos requemados,
y el suspirar de fuego
de los maduros campos.

    Tu hermana es clara y débil
como los juncos lánguidos,
como los sauces tristes,
como los linos glaucos.
Tu hermana es un lucero
en el azul lejano ...
Y es alba y aura fría
sobre los pobres álamos
que en las orillas tiemblan
del río humilde y manso.
Tu hermana es un lucero
en el azul lejano.

    De tu morena gracia,
de tu soñar gitano,
de tu mirar de sombra
quiero llenar mi vaso.
Me embriagaré una noche
de cielo negro y bajo,
para cantar contigo,
orilla al mar salado,

una canción que deje
cenizas en los labios ...
De tu mirar de sombra
quiero llenar mi vaso.

   Para tu linda hermana
arrancaré los ramos
de florecillas nuevas
a los almendros blancos,
en un tranquilo y triste
alborear de marzo.
Los regaré con agua
de los arroyos claros,
los ataré con verdes
junquillos del remanso ...
Para tu linda hermana
yo haré un ramito blanco.

Commentary

Based on the troubadour tradition of love as interpreted in the *cante* tradition of the late nineteenth century, especially in Seville, a tradition also glossed by Machado's contemporaries, the poem complements poem XXXVIII and, at the same time, echoes the longer popular tradition of dark and pale lovers.

   Published in *Blanco y Negro*, XIV, 699, 24-IX-1904 under the title 'Inventarios galantes / Canción'. Romancillo in 7s in e-a.

XLI

Me dijo una tarde
de la primavera:
Si buscas caminos
en flor en la tierra,
mata tus palabras
y oye tu alma vieja.
Que el mismo albo lino

que te vista, sea
tu traje de duelo,
tu traje de fiesta.
Ama tu alegría
y ama tu tristeza,
si buscas caminos
en flor en la tierra.
Respondí a la tarde
de la primavera:
Tú has dicho el secreto
que en mi alma reza:
Yo odio la alegría
por odio a la pena.
Mas antes que pise
tu florida senda,
quisiera traerte
muerta mi alma vieja.

Commentary

A further colloquy with a natural element: a spring afternoon. Once more, as in VII and XXXVII, an introspective dialogue of advice and reply on the question of lifestyle and poetic goals – listen to your youthful 'soul'; deny 'words' and listen to his 'alma vieja' or not? Note, once more, the religious terms employed: the poet as priest ('albo lino') and the advice to seek all emotions in his search. In his letter to Jiménez quoted in the Introduction he seeks a new poetic language as a means to 'regenerate' his spirit and that of the nation.

First entitled 'Ocaso' in 1903. Romancillo in 7s in e-a.

XLII

La vida hoy tiene ritmo
de ondas que pasan,
de olitas temblorosas
que fluyen y se alcanzan.

La vida hoy tiene el ritmo de los ríos,
la risa de las aguas
que entre los verdes junquerales corren,
y entre las verdes cañas.

Sueño florido lleva el manso viento;
bulle la savia joven en las nuevas ramas;
tiemblan alas y frondas,
y la mirada sagital del águila
no encuentra presa ... Treme el campo en sueños,
vibra el sol como un arpa.

¡Fugitiva ilusión de ojos guerreros,
que por las selvas pasas
a la hora del cenit: tiemble en mi pecho
el oro de tu aljaba!

En tus labios florece la alegría
de los campos en flor; tu veste alada
aroman las primeras velloritas,
las violetas perfuman tus sandalias.

Yo he seguido tus pasos en el viejo bosque,
arrebatados tras la corza rápida,
y los ágiles músculos rosados
de tus piernas silvestres entre verdes ramas.

¡Pasajera ilusión de ojos guerreros,
que por las selvas pasas
cuando la tierra reverdece y ríen
los ríos en las cañas!
¡Tiemble en mi pecho el oro
que llevas en tu aljaba!

Commentary

The poet evokes a pastoral idyll of harmony ('ritmo') with echoes of Parnassian and Decadent literary motifs typical of the late 1890s: see Cardwell 2009. Another influence might be Bécquer's *leyenda,* 'La corza blanca'. Machado contrasts time (flowing water) and breezes (dreams) in a symbolic landscape (the poet 'dreams' not the countryside) based on the reality of the environs of Soria. He recreates the figure of fleeting classical figures in Greek dress, *chiton*, possibly Diana the huntress and her attendants, who bring a sense of harmony (see XXV) but can also destroy ('ojos guerreros'). Are these Greek figures also the Muses as in poem XCI? He is struck by a golden arrow, symbol of inspiration. In a revision of the Cupid myth and the *saeta* of the Virgin Mary, he suggests, as with the springtime air, a new life in the form of inspiration, but one that wounds. The springtime symbolises a new birth of hope with the rider that the Muse/Diana is a 'pasajera ilusión'.

Published in *Revista Ibérica*, 4, 1902 under the title 'Salmodias de abril' and revised in *SGOP*. Silva romance in a-a with variants.

XLIII

Era una mañana y abril sonreía.
Frente al horizonte dorado moría
la luna, muy blanca y opaca; tras ella,
cual tenue ligera quimera, corría
la nube que apenas enturbia una estrella.

* * *

Como sonreía la rosa mañana
al sol del Oriente abrí mi ventana;
y en mi triste alcoba penetró el Oriente
en canto de alondras, en risa de fuente
y en suave perfume de flora temprana.

Fue una clara tarde de melancolía.
Abril sonreía. Yo abrí las ventanas
de mi casa al viento ... El viento traía
perfume de rosas, dolor de campanas ...

Doblar de campanas lejanas, llorosas,
suave de rosas aromado aliento ...
... ¿Dónde están los huertos floridos de rosas?
¿Qué dicen las dulces campanas al viento?

Pregunté a la tarde de abril que moría:
¿Al fin la alegría se acerca a mi casa?
La tarde de abril sonrió: La alegría
pasó por tu puerta —y luego, sombría:
Pasó por tu puerta. Dos veces no pasa.

Commentary

Based on the classical trope of 'Ubi sunt?' and the French poet Ronsard, a favourite of Machado. He again evokes springtime as the potential for inspiration. Note his skill in evoking a natural scene, one portrayed from a window (Symbolist frame) from which he experiences a series of sensual effects, especially the sound of bells, yet it is his 'dolor' not that of the bells. The poem, first entitled 'Mai più' (from Edgar Allan Poe's 'Nevermore') rather echoes Poe's 'The Bells', both poems forming the inspiration from the 1880s and 1890s for many Decadent expressions. The answer to the final question, in an echo of poem I and others, is negative. His early happiness cannot be recovered. For the 'Nevermore' motif see Ribbans 1971, 151–8 and 274–6; Gutiérrez García 2008 and Romero López 2013. 'Mai più' in *Soledades*.

Rhymed serventesios.

XLIV

El casco roído y verdoso
del viejo falucho
reposa en la arena ...
La vela tronchada parece
que aun sueña en el sol y en el mar.

El mar hierve y canta ...
El mar es un sueño sonoro
bajo el sol de abril.
El mar hierve y ríe
con olas azules y espumas de leche y de plata,
el mar hierve y ríe
bajo el cielo azul.

El mar lactescente,
el mar rutilante,
que ríe en sus liras de plata sus risas azules ...
¡Hierve y ríe el mar! ...

El aire parece que duerme encantado
en la fúlgida niebla de sol blanquecino.
La gaviota palpita en el aire dormido, y al lento
volar soñoliento, se aleja y se pierde en la bruma del sol.

Commentary

The sea setting is rare in *SGOP*, perhaps inspired by the marine paintings of Joaquín Soralla, the Spanish Impressionist and friend of Machado at this time, or the impact of Parnassianism. There is no record of a visit by Machado to the coast in this period. He takes delight in the movement of the sea, but the terms 'dormido' and 'duerme' suggest a hidden beauty beyond the reality transformed into a dream: 'sueño sonoro', 'aire dormido' and 'volar soñoliento'. Note also the ellipses, equivalent of longing or a sigh. 'La mar alegre' in *Soledades*.

A mixture of 6-, 9- and 11-syllable lines.

XLV

El sueño bajo el sol que aturde y ciega,
tórrido sueño en la hora de arrebol;
el río luminoso el aire surca;
esplende la montaña;
la tarde es polvo y sol.

El sibilante caracol del viento
ronco dormita en el remoto alcor;
emerge el sueño ingrave en la palmera,
luego se enciende en el naranjo en flor.

La estúpida cigüeña
su garabato escribe en el sopor
del molino parado; el toro abate
sobre la hierba la testuz feroz.

La verde, quieta espuma del ramaje
efunde sobre el blanco paredón,
lejano, inerte, del jardín sombrío,
dormido bajo el cielo fanfarrón.

   * * *

   Lejos, enfrente de la tarde roja,
refulge el ventanal del torreón.

Commentary

An early poem of 1901 containing terms like 'esplende', 'efunde', 'ingrave', refulge', which later verses eschew, words redolent of Decadent and Parnassian writing. See also 'lactescente', 'rutilante' and others in the previous poem. Machado creates a dreamlike landscape of heat and blinding light (as in Sorolla's paintings) where natural objects like the wind – 'el sibilante caracol del viento' – become plastic, the sound of the wind is transformed into the sound heard in a seashell, Parnassian and Symbolist effects combined. The landscape, probably of Andalucía, becomes a moodscape of listlessness since palm trees do not 'dream' nor gardens 'sleep'. This poem is very pictorial, reminiscent of the canvasses of Vázquez Díaz, Zuloaga and Solana, the emergent painters of the time, known to Machado. See Havard 2007. And Litvak 1998.

   Published in *Electra*, 6, 21-IV-1901 under the title 'Del camino' and revised in *SGOP*; 'Tierra baja' in *Soledades*. Silva romance in 16 and three 7s.

Humorismos, fantasías, apuntes: los grandes inventos

XLVI

(LA NORIA)

La tarde caía
triste y polvorienta.

El agua cantaba
su copla plebeya
en los cangilones
de la noria lenta.

Soñaba la mula,
¡pobre mula vieja!,
al compás de sombra
que en el agua suena.

La tarde caía
triste y polvorienta.

Yo no sé qué noble,
divino poeta,
unió a la amargura
de la eterna rueda

la dulce armonía
del agua que sueña,
y vendó tus ojos
¡pobre mula vieja! ...

Mas sé que fue un noble,
divino poeta,
corazón maduro
de sombra y de ciencia.

Commentary

The afternoon and the 'noria' become symbols of the poet himself. It is not the 'tarde' that is 'triste', nor the 'mula', nor does the water 'dream', rather the poet. Thus Machado creates another moodscape. The finale draws a conclusion of stoicism and heedless endeavour in an echo of an unnamed poet, possibly one of the Greek stoics or the philosopher Pythagoras whom Machado is constantly to invoke. Stoicism in the face of failing beliefs is a marked characteristic of Machado's work and this attitude forms part of his contribution to the respiritualisation of the nation.

Romancillo in 11s in e-a.

XLVII

(EL CADALSO)

La aurora asomaba
lejana y siniestra.
El lienzo de Oriente
sangraba tragedias,
pintarrajeadas
con nubes grotescas.

* * *

En la vieja plaza
de una vieja aldea,
erguía su horrible
pavura esquelética
el tosco patíbulo
de fresca madera ...

La aurora asomaba
lejana y siniestra.

Commentary

A rare poem where the scaffold becomes a picture ('lienzo') of a darker side of humanity. Perhaps Machado is thinking of various well-publicised trials and executions of terrorists in this period, sentences attacked by the intellectuals. Machado does not evoke the victim, rather the dawn that heralds his execution. Compare with Espronceda's 'El reo de muerte' of 1840.

Romancillo in 11 syllables in e-a.

XLVIII

(LAS MOSCAS)

Vosotras, las familiares,
inevitables golosas,
vosotras, moscas vulgares,
me evocáis todas las cosas.

¡Oh, viejas moscas voraces
como abejas en abril,
viejas moscas pertinaces
sobre mi calva infantil!

¡Moscas del primer hastío
en el salón familiar,
las claras tardes de estío
en que yo empecé a soñar!

Y en la aborrecida escuela,
raudas moscas divertidas,
perseguidas
por amor de lo que vuela,

—que todo es volar— sonoras
rebotando en los cristales
en los días otoñales ...
Moscas de todas las horas,
de infancia y adolescencia,
de mi juventud dorada;
de esta segunda inocencia,
que da en no creer en nada,

de siempre ... Moscas vulgares,
que de puro familiares
no tendréis digno cantor:
yo sé que os habéis posado
sobre el juguete encantado,
sobre el librote cerrado,
sobre la carta de amor,
sobre los párpados yertos
de los muertos.

Inevitables golosas,
que ni labráis como abejas
ni brilláis cual mariposas;
pequeñitas, revoltosas;
vosotras, amigas viejas,
me evocáis todas las cosas.

Commentary

The flies become the symbols of various stages of the poet's life, evoking memories. Machado, in drawing on such an unpoetic creature, becomes what his friend Azorín called the poet of 'lo nimio' in contemporary art. The flies become a symbol of the ordinary and quotidian, aspects Machado's generation were to depict in their art. See Reyes Vila-Belda 2004. The humoristic tone also recalls an amusing sonnet by Quevedo (1580–1645), 'Moscas de los sorbos finos'.

Romancillo in 11s in e-a.

XLIX

(ELEGÍA DE UN MADRIGAL)

Recuerdo que una tarde de soledad y hastío
¡oh tarde como tantas!, el alma mía era,
bajo el azul monótono, un ancho y terso río
que ni tenía un pobre juncal en su ribera.

¡Oh mundo sin encanto, sentimental inopia
que borra el misterioso azogue del cristal!
¡Oh el alma sin amores que el Universo copia
con un irremediable bostezo universal!

* * *

Quiso el poeta recordar a solas;
las ondas bien amadas, la luz de los cabellos
que él llamaba en sus rimas rubias olas.
Leyó ... La letra mata: no se acordaba de ellos ...

Y un día —como tantos— al aspirar un día
aromas de una rosa que en el rosal se abría,
brotó como una llama la luz de los cabellos
que él en sus madrigales llamaba rubias olas,
brotó, porque un aroma igual tuvieron ellos ...
Y se alejó en silencio para llorar a solas. (1907)

Commentary

The title is a contradiction: Madrigal is a short love song, Elegy mourns a death. Thus the poem mourns lost love and fulfilment. In the first section the poet evokes himself in terms of a wide, calm but barren river in a mood of 'soledad y hastío'. This world has lost its 'encanto', it is 'monótono'; the mysterious mirror to that lost world is steamed up and he experiences a universal tedium. Ribbans, in his editions of *SGOP*, has suggested that the second part seems unrelated to the first part. Yet the image of the clouded mirror (symbol of his frustrated search for a lost poetic world) fits with the idea of the poet here attempting to recapture lost memories, perhaps those of poem LXII, a constant motif in *SGOP*. Yet, when the poet comes to set those memories in words, those words are insufficient even though these powerful memories constantly recur. His inability to express these memories cause his withdrawl and his tears.

Alexandrine serventesios.

L

(ACASO ...)

Como atento no más a mi quimera
no reparaba en torno mío, un día
me sorprendió la fértil primavera
que en todo el ancho campo sonreía.

Brotaban verdes hojas,
de las hinchadas yemas del ramaje,
y flores amarillas, blancas, rojas,
alegraban la mancha del paisaje.

Y era una lluvia de saetas de oro,
el sol sobre las frondas juveniles;
del amplio río en el caudal sonoro
se miraban los álamos gentiles.

Tras de tanto camino es la primera
vez que miro brotar la primavera,
dije, y después, declamatoriamente:

— ¡Cuan tarde ya para la dicha mía! —
Y luego, al caminar, como quien siente
alas de otra ilusión: —Y todavía
¡yo alcanzaré mi juventud un día!

Commentary

One of the many spring poems where the new season inspires the poet with a longing for what has been lost. But the title and the ellipsis (a sigh, the 'perhaps') suggest doubt and nostalgia. These feelings, cast in natural terms, are accompanied by a new mood which evokes his lost youth (see poem I) and ends in an assertion of optimism. Note the intimate details of the flowers (the influence of the Institución Libre) and the sun expressed as 'una lluvia de saetas de oro', a complex metaphor which echoes not only the Virgin but more insistently, the mysterious huntress, a mixture of the relentless goddess, Diana, who destroys those who look on her, and the Muses who guard the golden

LII

(FANTASÍA DE UNA NOCHE DE ABRIL)

¿Sevilla?... ¿Granada?... La noche de luna,
blancas paredes y obscuras ventanas.
Cerrados postigos, corridas persianas...
El cielo vestía su gasa de abril.

Un vino risueño me dijo el camino.
Yo escucho los áureos consejos del vino,
el vino es a veces escala de ensueño.
Abril y la noche y el vino risueño
ataron en coro su salmo de amor.

La calle copiaba, con sombra en el muro,
el paso fantasma y el sueño maduro
de apuesto embozado, galán caballero:
espada tendida, calado sombrero...
La luna vertía su blanco soñar.

Como un laberinto mi sueño torcía
de calle en calleja. Mi sombra seguía
de aquel laberinto la sierpe encantada,
en pos de una oculta plazuela cerrada.
La luna lloraba su dulce blancor.

La casa y la clara ventana florida,
de blancos jazmines y nardos prendida,
más blancos que el blanco soñar de la luna...
—'Señora, la hora, tal vez importuna...
¿Que espere? (La dueña se lleva el candil.)

Ya sé que sería quimera, señora,
mi sombra galante buscando a la aurora
en noches de estrellas y luna, si fuera
mentira la blanca nocturna quimera
que usurpa a la luna su trono de luz.

¡Oh dulce señora, más cándida y bella
que la solitaria matutina estrella

fruit in the Woods of Helicon (see poems VI, VII and XCI), symbols of poetic inspiration. Thus inspiration is double-edged, it lures and yet can destroy, a major motif in Symbolist Decadent art.

Published in *Revista Latina*, 2, 30-X-1907. 11 syllable serventesios.

LI

(JARDÍN)

Lejos de tu jardín quema la tarde
inciensos de oro en purpurinas llamas,
tras el bosque de cobre y de ceniza.
En tu jardín hay dalias.
¡Malhaya tu jardín! ... Hoy me parece
la obra de un peluquero,
con esa pobre palmerilla enana,
y ese cuadro de mirtos recortados ...
y el naranjito en su tonel ... El agua
de la fuente de piedra
no cesa de reír sobre la concha blanca.

Commentary

A poem of disillusion. Once more Machado evokes a setting of light and heat. The vocabulary is markedly Decadent in its synaesthesia ('inciensos de oro', smell, colour – 'purpurinas' –, touch), and the use of metals and colour. But this Decadent garden (a standard motif in the *fin de siglo*) no longer holds its enchantment; all has shrunk, every plant is wrenched from its natural place in the earth or has been pruned of life. Even the fountain mocks him. Perhaps this poem is a critique of the artifice of the period but it is also a lament for a garden (symbol of former illusions and hopes) that he has lost or which has been ruined by artifice. Hence Machado's desire for a simpler form of expression.

Silva romance in a-a.

tan clara en el cielo! ¿Por qué silenciosa
oís mi nocturna querella amorosa?
¿Quién hizo, señora, cristal vuestra voz? ...

    La blanca quimera parece que sueña.
Acecha en la obscura estancia la dueña.
—Señora, si acaso otra sombra emboscada
teméis, en la sombra, fiad en mi espada ...
Mi espada se ha visto a la luna brillar.

    ¿Acaso os parece mi gesto anacrónico?
El vuestro es, señora, sobrado lacónico.
¿Acaso os asombra mi sombra embozada,
de espada tendida y toca plumada? ...
¿Seréis la cautiva del moro Gazul?

    Dijéraislo, y pronto mi amor os diría
el son de mi guzla y la algarabía
más dulce que oyera ventana moruna
Mi guzla os dijera la noche de luna,
la noche de cándida luna de abril.

    Dijera la clara cantiga de plata
del patio moruno, y la serenata
que lleva el aroma de floridas preces
a los miradores y a los ajimeces,
los salmos de un blanco fantasma lunar.

    Dijera las danzas de trenzas lascivas,
las muelles cadencias de ensueños, las vivas
centellas de lánguidos rostros velados,
los tibios perfumes, los huertos cerrados;
dijera el aroma letal del harén.

    Yo guardo, señora, en viejo salterio
también una copla de blanco misterio,
la copla más suave, más dulce y más sabia
que evoca las claras estrellas de Arabia
y aromas de un moro jardín andaluz.

Silencio ... En la noche la paz de la luna
alumbra la blanca ventana moruna.
Silencio ... Es el musgo que brota, y la hiedra
que lenta desgarra la tapia de piedra ...
El llanto que vierte la luna de abril.

—Si sois una sombra de la primavera
blanca entre jazmines, o antigua quimera
soñada en las trovas de dulces cantores,
yo soy una sombra de viejos cantares,
y el signo de un álgebra vieja de amores.

Los gayos, lascivos decires mejores,
los árabes albos nocturnos soñares,
las coplas mundanas, los salmos talares,
poned en mis labios;
yo soy una sombra también del amor.

Ya muerta la luna, mi sueño volvía
por la retorcida, moruna calleja.
El sol en Oriente reía
su risa más vieja.

Commentary

A joke poem and a pastiche of the poetry and themes of fellow poets of the period, fellow Andalusians who evoke the music, popular songs and manners of their homeland, probably Salvador Rueda, José Durbán Orozco or Francisco Villaespesa. He satirises not only the vogue for chivalric courtly love, but that for the vogue of the Arab presence in Andalusia, the exotic and the mysterious, all typical of much second-rank poetry of the *fin de siglo*. He also mocks his own poetic language, especially in stanza 9 with the *esdrújulo* rhyme, again reminiscent of Quevedo's comic-satiric verse. The story of the lover wandering the streets may be also pastiche of Espronceda's *El estudiante de Salamanca* (1840).

Published in *Renacimiento*, VIII, October 1907. In *Soledades* the poem was dedicated to his politician friend Eduardo Benot. Arte mayor of 12-syllable quintets followed by serventesios.

LIII

(A UN NARANJO Y A UN LIMONERO)
VISTOS EN UNA TIENDA DE PLANTAS Y FLORES

Naranjo en maceta, ¡qué triste es tu suerte!
Medrosas tiritan tus hojas menguadas.
Naranjo en la corte, ¡qué pena de verte
con tus naranjitas secas y arrugadas!

Pobre limonero de fruto amarillo
cual pomo pulido de pálida cera,
¡qué pena mirarte, mísero arbolito
criado en mezquino tonel de madera!

De los claros bosques de la Andalucía,
¿quién os trajo a esta castellana tierra
que barren los vientos de la adusta sierra,
hijos de los campos de la tierra mía?

¡Gloria de los huertos, árbol limonero,
que enciendes los frutos de pálido oro,
y alumbras del negro cipresal austero
las quietas plegarias erguidas en coro;
y fresco naranjo del patio querido,
del campo risueño y el huerto soñado,

siempre en mi recuerdo maduro o florido
de frondas y aromas y frutos cargado!

Commentary

As with the shrunken garden of poem LI, Machado again expresses his disillusion symbolically. The fruit trees, typical of Seville, his birthplace, stand in for the poet himself. He, like them, is in exile from his 'patio querido' in the Palacio de las Dueñas where he spent his childhood. At the same time the fruit are symbols of inspiration, associated with the Muses and the loss of poetic power (see poems VI, VII and XCI) for which he longs. Yet they are dry and withered.

Arte mayor 12-syllable serventesios.

LIV

(LOS SUEÑOS MALOS)

Está la plaza sombría;
muere el día.
Suenan lejos las campanas.

De balcones y ventanas
se iluminan las vidrieras,
con reflejos mortecinos,
como huesos blanquecinos
y borrosas calaveras.

En toda la tarde brilla
una luz de pesadilla.
Está el sol en el ocaso.
Suena el eco de mi paso.

—¿Eres tú? Ya te esperaba...
—No eres tú a quien yo buscaba.

Commentary

The menacing shadows of sunset and the tolling bells, sinister echoes and solitude create a sense of nightmare in this search for a lost presence. Elsewhere (in poem XCIV for example) the poet creates a similar feeling in his search for a lost goal.

Published in *Tierra soriana*, 16-VI-1908. Octosyllabic couplets with a rhyming redondilla in stanza 2.

LV

(HASTÍO)

Pasan las horas de hastío
por la estancia familiar,
el amplio cuarto sombrío
donde yo empecé a soñar.

Del reloj arrinconado,
que en la penumbra clarea,
el tictac acompasado
odiosamente golpea.
   Dice la monotonía
del agua clara al caer:
un día es como otro día;
hoy es lo mismo que ayer.

   Cae la tarde. El viento agita
el parque mustio y dorado ...
¡Qué largamente ha llorado
toda la fronda marchita!

Commentary

In this catalogue of elements of passing time, the clock, the falling rain, the wind, the autumn decay and a sense of sameness, Machado creates a symbol of his own 'hastío'. Various details reprise the mood in poem I.
   Redondillas.

LVI

   Sonaba el reloj la una,
dentro de mi cuarto. Era
triste la noche. La luna,
reluciente calavera,

   ya del cenit declinado,
iba del ciprés del huerto
fríamente iluminado
el alto ramaje yerto.

Por la entreabierta ventana
llegaban a mis oídos
metálicos alaridos
de una música lejana.

Una música tristona,
una mazurca olvidada,
entre inocente y burlona,
mal tañida y mal soplada.

Y yo sentí el estupor
del alma cuando bosteza
el corazón, la cabeza,
y ... morirse es lo mejor.

Commentary

Another evocation of his personal sadness and pessimism created by the familiar images of the chiming clock, the moon, the night (it is the poet who is sad, of course), the rigid cypress tree, the poorly played music of a mazurka (a parody of the Symbolist motif of distant music) etc. All these elements cause a sense of 'estupor' and the thoughts of death latent in the poet's mind.
Redondillas.

LVII

(CONSEJOS)

I
Este amor que quiere ser
acaso pronto será;
pero ¿cuándo ha de volver
lo que acaba de pasar?
Hoy dista mucho de ayer.
¡Ayer es Nunca jamás!

II
Moneda que está en la mano
quizá se deba guardar;
la monedita del alma
se pierde si no se da.

Commentary

Machado ecoes the *consejo* tradition established by Ramón de Campoamor in the 1830s which became popular across the century. Here he inserts an echo of Poe's 'Nevermore' and a gloss of his review of Unamuno's *Vida de don Quijote y Sancho* of 1905. See Ribbans 1971, 295–304.

Part I is an 8-syllable sextet, II a *copla*.

LVIII

(GLOSA)

    Nuestras vidas son los ríos,
que van a dar a la mar,
que es el morir. ¡Gran cantar!

    Entre los poetas míos
tiene Manrique un altar.

    Dulce goce de vivir:
mala ciencia del pasar,
ciego huir a la mar.

    Tras el pavor del morir
está el placer de llegar.

    ¡Gran placer!
Mas ¿y el horror de volver?
¡Gran pesar!

Commentary

Another gloss on traditional poetry, here the *coplas* of Jorge Manrique (1440–79) which Machado is to dwell on in later years. A major theme of popular verse was the river flowing to the sea as a metaphor for death and eternity. Here Machado, echoing a statement of his father in *Cantos populares españoles* (see Introduction), also meditates on the theme and the thought that a return would be painful.

This poem was added to *SGOP* after 1907. A gloss on a *villancico*.

LIX

Anoche cuando dormía
soñé, ¡bendita ilusión!
que una fontana fluía
dentro de mi corazón.

Di, ¿por qué acequia escondida,
agua, vienes hasta mi,
manantial de nueva vida
de donde nunca bebí?

Anoche cuando dormía
soñé, ¡bendita ilusión!
que una colmena tenía
dentro de mi corazón;
y las doradas abejas
iban fabricando en él,
con las amarguras viejas,
blanca cera y dulce miel.

Anoche cuando dormía
soñé, ¡bendita ilusión!
que un ardiente sol lucía
dentro de mi corazón.
Era ardiente porque daba
calores de rojo hogar,
y era sol porque alumbraba
y porque hacía llorar.

Anoche cuando dormía
soñé, ¡bendita ilusión!
que era Dios lo que tenía
dentro de mi corazón.

Commentary

One of the more optimistic poems of Machado's early verses, also added to *SGOP* later. Here Machado glosses the three theological virtues (faith, hope and charity) in the shape of the fountain, bees and the sun. At the same time these images suggest poetic practice: the flowing of inspiration, the conversion of negative aspects into positives and the illumination poetry brings, which suggest, in his dream, a union with God. Arguably, this is the only early poem where Machado senses His presence.

Another gloss on a *villancico* in redondilla form.

LX

¿Mi corazón se ha dormido?
Colmenares de mis sueños
¿ya no labráis? ¿Está seca
la noria del pensamiento,
los cangilones vacíos,
girando, de sombra llenos?
 No, mi corazón no duerme.
Está despierto, despierto.
Ni duerme ni sueña, mira,
los claros ojos abiertos,
señas lejanas y escucha
a orillas del gran silencio.

Commentary

By contrast with LIX, this poem denies the power of the three images of water, bees and sun, the latter now shade. For the moment the 'dream' (his inspiration) is lost, seeking 'señas lejanas' in the face of a 'gran silencio'. For a fuller unpublished manuscript version of this poem see Ribbans' editions of *SGOP*.

8-syllable romance in e-o.

Galerías

LXI

(INTRODUCCIÓN)

Leyendo un claro día
mis bien amados versos,
he visto en el profundo
espejo de mis sueños

que una verdad divina
temblando está de miedo,
y es una flor que quiere
echar su aroma al viento.

El alma del poeta
se orienta hacia el misterio.
Sólo el poeta puede
mirar lo que está lejos
dentro del alma, en turbio
y mago sol envuelto.

En esas galerías,
sin fondo, del recuerdo,
donde las pobres gentes
colgaron cual trofeo
el traje de una fiesta
apolillado y viejo,
allí el poeta sabe
el laborar eterno
mirar de las doradas
abejas de los sueños.

Poetas, con el alma
atenta al hondo cielo,
en la cruel batalla
o en el tranquilo huerto,
la nueva miel labramos

con los dolores viejos,
la veste blanca y pura
pacientemente hacemos,
y bajo el sol bruñimos
el fuerte arnés de hierro.

El alma que no sueña,
el enemigo espejo,
proyecta nuestra imagen
con un perfil grotesco.

Sentimos una ola
de sangre, en nuestro pecho,
que pasa ... y sonreímos,
y a laborar volvemos.

Commentary

The poem is a manifesto of and 'Introduction' to Machado's poetic practice and his view of the role of poetry in tune with his expressed views of its regenerative power in the letter to Jiménez. He employs the Symbolist motif of the mirror in which he describes a 'verdad divina', the pure 'Word' set out in St John's Gospel made aesthetic. He returns to the motif of 'mystery' and the hazards faced, already set out in part in earlier poems: blinding light, galleries, mirrors, play-acting, sincerity, etc. The final part of the poem expresses the ideals of the *Helios* group to 'regenerate' the spirit of the nation (see my Introduction) where the poet becomes a warrior ('arnés') and priest ('veste blanca'), a reprise of the sonnet Rubén Darío dedicated to Jiménez's *Ninfeas* of 1900 and the consequent conversion of the poet/writer into a national saviour, an ideal taken up by almost all the young writers of the time led by Unamuno. See Cardwell 1993. Without the dream, Machado senses, the mirror distorts the ideal, yet the poet must, for all the hazards, press on in his regenerative task.

Heptasyllabic romance in e-o.

LXII

    Desgarrada la nube; el arco iris
brillando ya en el cielo,
y en un fanal de lluvia
y sol en el campo envuelto.

    Desperté. ¿Quién enturbia
los mágicos cristales de mi sueño?
Mi corazón latía
atónito y disperso.

    ... ¡El limonar florido,
el cipresal del huerto,
el prado verde, el sol, el agua, el iris ...,
el agua en tus cabellos! ...

    Y todo en la memoria se perdía
como una pompa de jabón al viento.

Commentary

Machado evokes a moment of powerful memory as the clouds part to reveal a rainbow and a brilliant light in the rain. Here, as in tradition, the 'iris' is a symbol of the Covenant but expressed now in Symbolist terms of inspiration. His imagination, voiced again in an image of glass, is 'enturbiado', recalling a past springtime of love. Yet, like a soap bubble (which echoes the iridescence of the rainbow itself), his memory 'shines' and as quickly bursts, suggesting the precarious nature of poetic recall. Is this 'tú' the shadow, the 'ilusión cándida' he recalls in poem VII and elsewhere?

Published in *Helios*, II, IV, 14, May 1903 with the title 'Galerías'. Silva romance in e-o.

LXIII

    Y era el demonio de mi sueño, el ángel
más hermoso. Brillaban
como aceros los ojos victoriosos,
y las sangrientas llamas
de su antorcha alumbraron
la honda cripta del alma.

    — ¿Vendrás conmigo? —No, jamás; las tumbas
y los muertos me espantan.
Pero la férrea mano
mi diestra atenazaba.

    —Vendrás conmigo ... Y avancé en mi sueño
cegado por la roja luminaria.
Y en la cripta sentí sonar cadenas,
y rebullir de fieras enjauladas.

Commentary

Another attempt to evoke the dangerous nature of poetic inspiration in which the fleeting figure (lost beloved, the huntress, the Muses) becomes a demon/angel who lures the poet to an uncertain destiny in his imagination. Rather than the 'hora de ilusión' of poem XXV, he discovers a blinding light and the fear of incarceration in his mind.

    Published in *Helios*, I, II, xi, November 1903 under the title 'Galerías'. Silva romance in a-a.

LXIV

    Desde el umbral de un sueño me llamaron ...
Era la buena voz, la voz querida.

    —Dime: ¿vendrás conmigo a ver el alma? ...
Llegó a mi corazón una caricia.

    Contigo siempre ... Y avancé en mi sueño
por una larga, escueta galería,

sintiendo el roce de la veste pura
y el palpitar suave de la mano amiga.

Commentary

A complementary poem to number LXIII where the search for illumination finds a more positive outcome as the 'voz querida', dressed as a priestess ('veste pura'), leads the poet to his goal.

Published in *Helios*, I, II, xi, November 1903. 11 syllable romance in i-a.

LXV

(SUEÑO INFANTIL)

Una clara noche
de fiesta y de luna,
noche de mis sueños,
noche de alegría

   —era luz de mi alma,
que hoy es bruma toda,
no eran mis cabellos
negros todavía—,

   el hada más joven
me llevó en sus brazos
a la alegre fiesta
que en la plaza ardía.

So el chisporroteo
de las luminarias,
amor sus madejas
de danzas tejía.

   Y en aquella noche
de fiesta y de luna,
noche de mis sueños,
noche de alegría,

el hada más joven
besaba mi frente ...,
con su linda mano
su adiós me decía ...

   Todos los rosales
daban sus aromas,
todos los amores
amor entreabría.

Commentary

Employing a childhood dream of a fairground and fiesta, evoked again in XCII, he contrasts the 'luz', experienced then, with his present. He recalls his muse and the night of 'sueños' and 'alegría' where powerful scents and love dominated. But it is only a dream.

   Published in *Helios*, I, II, xi, November 1903 under the title 'Tristezas' (accompanied by poems LXVIII and LXIX). Hexasyllables with free verses.

LXVI

   Y esos niños en hilera,
llevando el sol de la tarde
en sus velitas de cera! ...

      * * *

   ¡De amarilla calabaza,
en el azul, cómo sube
la luna, sobre la plaza!

      * * *

   Duro ceño.
Pirata, rubio africano,
barbitaheño.

      * * *

Lleva un alfanje en la mano.
Estas figuras del sueño ...

   * * *

Donde las niñas cantan en corro,
en los jardines del limonar,
sobre la fuente, negro abejorro
pasa volando, zumba al volar.

Se oyó un bronco gruñir de abuelo
entre las claras voces sonar,
superflua nota de violoncelo
en los jardines del limonar.

Entre las cuatro blancas paredes,
cuando una mano cerró el balcón,
por los salones de sal-si-puedes
suena el rebato de su bordón.

Muda en el techo, quieta, ¿dormida?
la negra nota de angustia está,
y en la pradera verdiflorida
de un sueño niño volando va ...

Commentary

Strictly speaking this poem was not included in the 1907 *SGOP*. It appeared in the 1936 edition of the complete poems. I include it here since it belongs to Machado's continued interest in popular poetry following the enormous influence of his father and grandmother. Each of these verses echo traditional folksong measures, usually sung to the guitar and accompanied by the one-string *bordón*, the poem a type of *cante* employing powerful images of domestic scenes with music, fiestas, Arab influence, gardens, childhood which Machado seems to recall in the final line.

  Two soleares, a quintilla and four 10-syllable serventesios.

LXVII

　　Si yo fuera un poeta
galante cantaría
a vuestros ojos un cantar tan puro
como en el mármol blanco el agua limpia.

　　Y en una estrofa de agua
todo el cantar sería:

　　'Ya sé que no responden a mis ojos,
que ven y no preguntan cuando miran,
los vuestros claros, vuestros ojos tienen
la buena luz tranquila,
la buena luz del mundo en flor, que he visto
desde los brazos de mi madre un día.'

Commentary

The poem glosses the love poetry tradition of the early Renaissance. Here Machado desires to be a love poet and evokes something of poems VII and LXII where an early love and his mother are recalled. Arguably Machado uses the gaze here to symbolise the search for his ideal. Many poems employ a gaze as the path for his search.

　　Published in *Helios*, II, IV, 14, May 1904 entitled 'Madrigal' and epigraph: 'Ojos claros, serenos ... CETINA'. The final section glosses this madrigal by Gutierre de Cetina (1520–157?), an early Renaissance poet. Silva romance in i-a.

LXVIII

　　Llamó a mi corazón, un claro día,
con un perfume de jazmín, el viento.

　　—A cambio de este aroma,
todo el aroma de tus rosas quiero.
　　—No tengo rosas; flores
en mi jardín no hay ya; todas han muerto.

Me llevaré los llantos de las fuentes,
las hojas amarillas y los mustios pétalos.
Y el viento huyó ... Mi corazón sangraba
Alma, ¿qué has hecho de tu pobre huerto?

Commentary

Another colloquy with an inanimate object, the wind, promising the scents of youth, which finally flees. The desired object, here symbolised by the perfume of the roses, is denied him. All that he can take from this dying garden is withered leaves and flowers. Cast as a barren orchard (absence of golden fruit), he suffers in his loss.

Published in *Helios*, I, II, xi, November 1903 under the title 'Tristezas'. Silva romance in e-o.

LXIX

Hoy buscarás en vano
a tu dolor consuelo.

Lleváronse tus hadas
el lino de tus sueños.
Está la fuente muda,
y está marchito el huerto.
Hoy sólo quedan lágrimas
para llorar. No hay que llorar, ¡silencio!

Commentary

Addressing himself, he evokes an inconsolable 'dolor'. His muses have left him without dreams, the fountain and the orchard (his ideal symbolic space), are silent and decayed. Note the use of 'lino' (canvas), in tune with Machado's use of pictures, canvases and other 'spaces' and 'frames'. There remains no screen for images, merely silence, the absence of words.

Published in *Helios*, I, II, ix, November 1903 with poem LXVII under the title 'Tristezas'. Heptasyllabic romance in e-o with the final line a seguidilla.

LXX

Y nada importa ya que el vino de oro
rebose de tu copa cristalina,
o el agrio zumo enturbie el puro vaso ...

Tú sabes, las secretas galerías
del alma, los caminos de los sueños,
y la tarde tranquila
donde van a morir ... Allí te aguardan

las hadas silenciosas de la vida,
y hacia un jardín de eterna primavera
te llevarán un día.

Commentary

Again in a self-address, Machado returns to Anacreon (see XXVIII) but uses the wine motif to symbolise inspiration, the substance and container of his imagination. The 'vino de oro', pressed from the Muses' 'frutos de oro', offer a means to his desired realm symbolised in the poetic version and reprise of Eden, of classical Paradise, 'el jardín de eternal primavera', timeless and flowering.

Helios, I, II, xi, November 1903, entitled 'Galerías', last of a set of poems under this heading. Silva romance in i-a. See the note to poem VI for essays on Machado's Paradise.

LXXI

Tocados de otros días,
mustios encajes y marchitas sedas;
salterios arrumbados,
rincones de las salas polvorientas;

daguerrotipos turbios,
cartas que amarillean;
libracos no leídos
que guardan grises florecitas secas;

    romanticismos muertos,
cursilerías viejas,
cosas de ayer que sois el alma, y cantos
y cuentos de la abuela! ...

Commentary

In a list of faded and ageing objects discovered in a symbolic attic are recalled and associated with the popular songs and folktales of his grandmother heard in childhood and, thus, stand in for the very 'soul' of the past and of Spain. Yet the Decadent tone of faded objects and *bibelots*, reminiscent of the early work of Valle-Inclán, a friend, and the Frech Decadence, suggests that Spain, like these relics, lives on the past.
Silva romance in e-a.

LXXII

    La casa tan querida
donde habitaba ella,
sobre un montón de escombros arruinada
o derruida, enseña
el negro y carcomido
mal trabado esqueleto de madera.

    La luna está vertiendo
su clara luz en sueños que platea
en las ventanas. Mal vestido y triste,
voy caminando por la calle vieja.

Commentary

The ruined home and the absent 'ella', together with the self-description, 'mal vestido y triste' create a 'moodscape' where the moon, like the poet, 'dreams'. Perhaps the lost house and the lost 'ella' symbolise his lost world of the imagination and, at the same time, the poverty of Spain itself.
Silva romance in e-a.

LXXIII

Ante el pálido lienzo de la tarde,
la iglesia, con sus torres afiladas
y el ancho campanario, en cuyos huecos
voltean suavemente las campanas,
alta y sombría, surge.

La estrella es una lágrima
en el azul celeste.
Bajo la estrella clara,
flota, vellón disperso,
una nube quimérica de plata.

Commentary

Once more the 'frame' of a 'lienzo', a screen onto which Machado projects his feelings, here the ancient church and the night sky, a timeless 'soul' of Spain (see poems III, VIII and XXXI).
Silva romance in a-a.

LXXIV

Tarde tranquila, casi
con placidez de alma,
para ser joven, para haberlo sido
cuando Dios quiso, para
tener algunas alegrías ... lejos,
y poder dulcemente recordarlas.

Commentary

A poem of nostalgia set in another 'moodscape', the poet feels the 'placidez', recalling what he lists as lost in poem I. See also LXXXVII, LXXXVIII and LXXXIX where, again, his spirits appear at a low ebb.
Silva romance in a-a.

LXXV

Yo, como Anacreonte,
quiero cantar, reír y echar al viento
las sabias amarguras
y los graves consejos,

y quiero, sobre todo, emborracharme,
ya lo sabéis ... ¡Grotesco!
Pura fe en el morir, pobre alegría
y macabro danzar antes de tiempo.

Commentary

Another gloss on the Anacreontic bacchic poem tradition, the 'musa risueña' of the verses of poet acquaintances of the 1900s. Thoughts of death are lulled by wine, a 'pobre alegría'. Machado, in the early 1900s was known for his love of alcohol. By his contact with the *Helios* group in 1902–3 he appears to have had second thoughts.

Silva romance in a-a.

LXXVI

¡Oh tarde luminosa!
El aire está encantado.
La blanca cigüeña
dormita volando,
y las golondrinas se cruzan, tendidas
las alas agudas al viento dorado,
y en la tarde risueña se alejan
volando, soñando ...

Y hay una que torna como la saeta,
las alas agudas tendidas al aire sombrío,
buscando su negro rincón del tejado.

La blanca cigüeña,
como un garabato,
tranquila y disforme, ¡tan disparatada!
sobre el campanario.

Commentary

Another, more optimistic 'moodscape': the 'tarde' cannot smile nor dream, only the poet. Note the detailed observation of the birds, part of lessons learned in the Institución walks in the countryside as a schoolboy. He attempts a picture of a timeless afternoon of Spain, probably his native Andalucía, though some have argued for Soria.

Romance in e-a with variations of 6-, 7-, 10- and 12-syllable lines.

LXXVII

Es una tarde cenicienta y mustia,
destartalada, como el alma mía;
y es esta vieja angustia
que habita mi usual hipocondría.

La causa de esta angustia no consigo
ni vagamente comprender siquiera;
pero recuerdo y, recordando, digo:
—Sí, yo era niño, y tú, mi compañera.

* * *

Y no es verdad, dolor, yo te conozco,
tú eres nostalgia de la vida buena
y soledad de corazón sombrío,
de barco sin naufragio y sin estrella.

Como perro olvidado que no tiene
huella ni olfato y yerra
por los caminos, sin camino, como
el niño que en la noche de una fiesta

se pierde entre el gentío
y el aire polvoriento y las candelas
chispeantes, atónito, y asombra
su corazón de música y de pena,

así voy yo, borracho melancólico,
guitarrista lunático, poeta,

y pobre hombre en sueños,
siempre buscando a Dios entre la niebla.

Commentary

Here the afternoon is 'like' the poem's theme rather than a *paysage d'âme*; it mirrors his 'vieja angustia'. Once more he probes his feelings and memories to conclude that, even as a child, he felt this mood, one of doubt and the desire for some undefined ideal. Compare the sentiments in poem I. He portrays himself in a series of images of loss and recreates the image of the child in the fairground he evokes elsewhere (LXV). He concludes in a reprise of the failed actor and a dreamer in search of a faith. See Wilcox 1985.

A form of romance in a-o with variants of 6-, 7-, 10- and 12-syllable lines.

LXXVIII

¿Y ha de morir contigo el mundo
donde guarda el recuerdo
los hálitos más puros de la vida,
la blanca sombra del amor primero,

la voz que fue a tu corazón, la mano
que tú querías retener en sueños,
y todos los amores
que llegaron al alma, al hondo cielo?

¿Y ha de morir contigo el mundo tuyo,
la vieja vida en orden tuyo y nuevo?
¿Los yunques y crisoles de tu alma
trabajan para el polvo y para el viento?

Commentary

A haunting question that runs subliminally through this collection: do all the wonderful memories of life die with the poet? This world is 'puro', made of 'sueños' and 'amores', the very things these poems seek to define or capture. Note the image of the forge ('yunque', 'crisol') which suggests alchemy and also the forging of a new art in tune with the *Helios* idealism.

Silva romance in e-o with 7 and 11 syllables.

LXXIX

Desnuda está la tierra,
y el alma aúlla al horizonte pálido
como loba famélica. ¿Qué buscas,
poeta, en el ocaso?

Amargo caminar, porque el camino
pesa en el corazón. ¡El viento helado,
y la noche que llega, y la amargura
de la distancia! ... En el camino blanco

algunos yertos árboles negrean;
en los montes lejanos
hay oro y sangre ... El sol murió... ¿Qué buscas
poeta, en el ocaso?

Commentary

A bleak landscape frames the poet's questioning, the 'camino', symbolising the perilous journey and the uncertainty experienced in his search for his goal, as often, over the horizon. Note the contrast here of negative elements (cold wind, gathering darkness, distant, rigid trees, etc.) with other poems of evoked springtime.

Silva romance in a-o with 7 and 11 syllables.

LXXX

(CAMPO)

La tarde está muriendo
como un hogar humilde que se apaga.

Allá, sobre los montes,
quedan algunas brasas.

Y ese árbol roto en el camino blanco
hace llorar de lástima.

¡Dos ramas en el tronco herido, y una
hoja marchita y negra en cada rama!

¿Lloras?... Entre los álamos de oro,
lejos, la sombra del amor te aguarda.

Commentary

Again the sunset and the damaged tree become the bearers of the poet's mood, one near to tears. Yet, once more, Machado evokes the 'álamos de oro', symbol of the Woods of Helicon and the Muses (see XCI) where his poetic dream awaits him.

Published in *Helios*, I, III, ii, February 1904 under the title 'Impresiones de otoño' along with poem LXXXI. Note again the painterly quality of this and the next poem. Silva romance in a-a in 11 and 7s.

LXXXI

(A UN VIEJO Y DISTINGUIDO SEÑOR)

Te he visto, por el parque ceniciento
que los poetas aman
para llorar, cómo una noble sombra
vagar, envuelto en tu levita larga.

El talante cortés, ha tantos años
compuesto de una fiesta en la antesala,
¡qué bien tus pobres huesos
ceremoniosos guardan!

Yo te he visto, aspirando distraído,
con el aliento que la tierra exhala
—hoy tibia tarde en que las mustias hojas
húmedo viento arranca—,

del eucalipto verde
el frescor de las hojas perfumadas.
Y te he visto llevar la seca mano
a la perla que brilla en tu corbata.

Commentary

In this 'moodscape' of autumnal decay ('parque ceniciento', 'mustias hojas') Machado createts a *contrafigura*. He, like the old man in his dated attire (the pearl in the cravat), seeks what has been lost to time, 'hojas perfumadas'. This poem, like LXXX, has the feel of a painting, here an Impressionist canvas.

Published in *Helios*, I, III, ii, February 1904 under the title 'Impresiones de otoño' with poem LXXX. Silva romance in a-a in 7 and 11 syllables.

LXXXII

(LOS SUEÑOS)

El hada más hermosa ha sonreído
al ver la lumbre de una estrella pálida,
que en hilo suave, blanco y silencioso
se enrosca al huso de su rubia hermana.

Y vuelve a sonreír, porque en su rueca
el hilo de los campos se enmaraña.
Tras la tenue cortina de la alcoba
está el jardín envuelto en luz dorada.

La cuna, casi en sombra. El niño duerme.
Dos hadas laboriosas lo acompañan,
hilando de los sueños los sutiles
copos en ruecas de marfil y plata.

Commentary

An attempt to define his dreams, here through a fairy story, a theme popular at the time, especially in the work of his *Helios* friend Gregorio

Martínez Sierra. The 'hada' is the poet's Muse who, like the poet, stares at the stars and is involved in a spinning image, symbolic threads which will compose the future of the child in the cradle, defined by the Fates. The magic causes, through the 'frame' of the curtains, the symbolic garden, the desired place, to fill with golden light, again a reference to the Golden Woods.Thus, the poet, like the child overlooked by other muses, has his dreams engendered.

Published in *Helios*, II, III, ii, February 1904, entitled 'Galerías'. 11-syllable romance in a-a.

LXXXIII

Guitarra del mesón que hoy suenas jota,
mañana petenera,
según quien llega y tañe
las empolvadas cuerdas,

guitarra del mesón de los caminos,
no fuiste nunca, ni serás, poeta.

Tú eres alma que dice su armonía
solitaria a las almas pasajeras ...

Y siempre que te escucha el caminante
sueña escuchar un aire de su tierra.

Commentary

The popular folk music of the guitar played in public gatherings may not be high art but it and the guitar represent the the 'soul' of the nation. Each who hears it 'dreams' of his *patria chica*.

Published in *La República de las Letras*, I, 3, 20-V-1905 under the title 'Del camino'. Silva romance in e-o.

LXXXIV

   El rojo sol de un sueño en el Oriente asoma.
Luz en sueños. ¿No tiemblas, andante peregrino?
Pasado el llano verde, en la florida loma,
acaso está el cercano final de tu camino.

   Tú no verás del trigo la espiga sazonada
y de macizas pomas cargado el manzanar,
ni de la vid rugosa la uva aurirrosada
ha de exprimir su alegre licor en tu lagar.

   Cuando el primer aroma exhalen los jazmines
y cuando más palpiten las rosas del amor,
una mañana de oro que alumbre los jardines,
¿no huirá, como una nube dispersa, el sueño en flor?

   Campo recién florido y verde, ¡quién pudiera
soñar aún largo tiempo en estas pequeñitas
corolas azuladas que manchan la pradera,
y en esas diminutas primeras margaritas!

Commentary

The setting sun, as in many of these poems, becomes the initiator of a dream sequence, 'luz en sueños', and the 'peregrino' (note the religious tone), an alter ego, is addressed by Machado himself. Again, with a reverse version of the Psalms, the 'tú' is told that he will never receive the reward of his dreams; the harvest of corn, fruit and grape will never come. At the very point of flowering his dream will melt away. The conditional of impossibility – quién pudiera' – suggests that, for all the spring growth, the dream is unattainable. Again a possible echo of Ronsard's lament for lost ideals. Ronsard was a favourite poet of Machado. See poem XVIII. Note the details of the wild flowers, the product of Machado's contact with nature during his education in the Institución.

   Published in *Blanco y Negro*, XV, 759, 18-XI-1905 under the title 'Presentimientos'. Alexandrine serventesios.

LXXXV

    La primavera besaba
suavemente la arboleda,
y el verde nuevo brotaba
como una verde humareda.

    Las nubes iban pasando
sobre el campo juvenil ...
Yo vi en las hojas temblando
las frescas lluvias de abril.

    Bajo ese almendro florido,
todo cargado de flor
—recordé—, yo he maldecido
mi juventud sin amor.

    Hoy, en mitad de la vida,
me he parado a meditar ...
¡Juventud nunca vivida
quién te volviera a soñar!

Commentary

One of several poems where the mature Machado – about 29 or 30 years old – reflects on his earlier life. In a possible echo of Dante's 'nel mezzo del camin di nostra vita' he reiterates the sentiments of poem I reflecting on the lost possibilities of youth made the more poignant by the flush of springtime.
    Redondillas.

LXXXVI

    Eran ayer mis dolores
como gusanos de seda
que iban labrando capullos;
hoy son mariposas negras.

¡De cuántas flores amargas
ha sacado blanca cera!
¡Oh tiempo en que mis pesares
trabajaban como abejas!

Hoy son como avenas locas,
o cizaña en sementera,
como tizón en espiga,
como carcoma en madera.

¡Oh tiempo en que mis dolores
tenían lágrimas buenas,
y eran como agua de noria
que va regando una huerta!
Hoy son agua de torrente
que arranca el limo a la tierra.

Dolores que ayer hicieron
de mi corazón colmena,
hoy tratan mi corazón
como a una muralla vieja:
quieren derribarlo, y pronto,
al golpe de la piqueta.

Commentary

Once more the theme of lost illusions set in past/present contrasts with the former also associated with 'dolor' in a break with the Romantic 'el bien pasado, el dolor presente' (Espronceda), see poem VI. Yet the past brought 'lágrimas buenas', while the present is hostile. Machado seems to find a sort of consolation in his 'dolor'. It was a common theme in this period, witness Azorín: 'El dolor es bello; él da al hombre el más intenso estado de conciencia; él hace meditar; él nos saca de la perdurable frivolidad humana' (1902: I, 890). And Unamuno: 'este nobilísimo, y el más profundo, y el más humano, y el más fecundo estado de alma, el de la desesperación. ... Y han hecho del arte una religión y un remedio para el mal metafísico' (*O.C.*, 1911: XVI, 178–9).

This is a late poem and did not appear in the first edition of *SGOP*. Romance in e-a.

LXXXVII

(RENACIMIENTO)

    Galería del alma... ¡El alma niña!
Su clara luz risueña;
y la pequeña historia,
y la alegría de la vida nueva ...

    ¡Ah, volver a nacer, y andar camino,
ya recobrada la perdida senda!

    Y volver a sentir en nuestra mano
aquel latido de la mano buena
de nuestra madre ... Y caminar en sueños
por amor de la mano que nos lleva.

    * * *

En nuestras almas todo
por misteriosa mano se gobierna.
Incomprensibles, mudas,
nada sabemos de las almas nuestras.

    Las más hondas palabras
del sabio nos enseñan,
lo que el silbar del viento cuando sopla,
o el sonar de las aguas cuando ruedan.

Commentary

Inner feelings are depicted as 'galerías del alma', a symbolic space or frame which is associated with his early years, even the embrace of his mother earlier evoked in poem VII, a time of undivided wholeness. Hence the longing to return to this desired state. The second part reflects on life's enigmas and the 'sabio's' lesson, which he seems to accept stoically. The rule of time is symbolised in the wind and running water. Machado does not identify the 'sabio'.

    Published in *Renacimiento Latino*, I, 1 April 1905. The second part of the poem appeared in *Revista latina*, I, 2, 30-X-1907, entitled 'Galerías'. Silva romance in e-a in 11s and 7s.

LXXXVIII

    Tal vez la mano, en sueños,
del sembrador de estrellas,
hizo sonar la música olvidada

    como una nota de la lira inmensa,
y la ola humilde a nuestros labios vino
de unas pocas palabras verdaderas.

Commentary

The Neo-Platonic idea of the music of the spheres is employed to express the search for inspiration, 'unas pocas palabras verdaderas' heard from a 'lira inmensa', an idea common among his poet friends and found in his reading of San Juan de la Cruz and Fray Luis de León, poets of the sixteenth century, as well as the Greek philosopher Pythagoras whom Machado comments on regularly.
    Published in *Revista Latina*, I, 2, 30-X-1907 under the title 'Galerías' with poem LXXXVII. Silva romance in e-a in 11s and 7s.

LXXXIX

    Y podrás conocerte, recordando
del pasado soñar los turbios lienzos,
en este día triste en que caminas
con los ojos abiertos.

    De toda la memoria, sólo vale
el don preclaro de evocar los sueños.

Commentary

Machado suggests that through a hazy memory and dream a real self-knowledge can be gained ('con los ojos abiertos'). This sentiment is in tune with the ideas of the *Helios* group who sought a spiritual identity through Art. Note again the use of the Symbolist 'frame': 'lienzo'.

Published in *Revista Latina*, I, 2, 30-X-1907 under the title 'Galerías' with LXXXVII and LXXXVIII. Silva romance in 11s and 7s.

XC

Los árboles conservan
verdes aun las copas,
pero del verde mustio
de las marchitas frondas.

El agua de la fuente,
sobre la piedra tosca
y de verdín cubierta,
resbala silenciosa.

Arrastra el viento algunas
amarillentas hojas.
¡El viento de la tarde
sobre la tierra en sombra!

Commentary

An evocation of time and passing time in the autumnal effects of dried leaves, moss, the wind and lengthening shadows.

Published in *Revista Latina*, I, 2, 30-X-1907, the fourth poem in the series 'Galerías', with the preceding three poems. Romance in 6s in o-a.

XCI

Húmedo está, bajo el laurel, el banco
de verdinosa piedra;
lavó la lluvia, sobre el muro blanco,
las empolvadas hojas de la hiedra.

Del viento del otoño el tibio aliento
los céspedes undula, y la alameda

conversa con el viento ...
¡el viento de la tarde en la arboleda!

    Mientras el sol en el ocaso esplende
que los racimos de la vid orea,
y el buen burgués, en su balcón, enciende
la estoica pipa en que el tabaco humea,

    voy recordando versos juveniles ...
¿Qué fue de aquel mi corazón sonoro?
¿Será cierto que os vais, sombras gentiles,
huyendo entre los árboles de oro?

Commentary

See the commentary of this poem in the Appendix.
    Published in *Revista Latina*, I, 2, 30-X-1907 under the title 'Galerías' with the preceding four poems. 11-syllable serventesios.

Varia

XCII

'Tournez, tournez, chevaux de bois.'
                           VERLAINE.

Pegasos, lindos pegasos,
caballitos de madera.

Yo conocí, siendo niño,
la alegría de dar vueltas
sobre un corcel colorado,
en una noche de fiesta.

En el aire polvoriento
chispeaban las candelas,
y la noche azul ardía
toda sembrada de estrellas.

¡Alegrías infantiles
que cuestan una moneda
de cobre, lindos pegasos,
caballitos de madera!

Commentary

Machado misquotes Verlaine, whom he met in Paris in 1899. The quotation should read: 'Tournez, tournez, bons chevaux de bois –', in the section 'Chevaux de bois' from *Romance sans paroles* and again in *Sagesse*. He uses the fairground motif once more (see LXV and LXXVII) to recall the pleasure of childhood, time for which Machado longs.

Traditional romance in e-a in 8 syllables.

XCIII

Deletreos de armonía
que ensaya inexperta mano.

Hastío. Cacofonía
del sempiterno piano
que yo de niño escuchaba
soñando ... no sé con qué.

Con algo que no llegaba,
todo lo que ya se fue.

Commentary

Machado recalls his dreams of childhood to the sound of poorly played music, possibly a symbol of his own mature art or a corruption of the celestial music of the spheres. Yet the dream never gained substance and has disappeared leaving only the earlier 'hastío'.
Published in *Renacimiento*, I, March 1907 under the title 'Ruidos'. Redondillas.

XCIV

En medio de la plaza y sobre tosca piedra,
el agua brota y brota. En el cercano huerto
eleva, tras el muro ceñido por la hiedra,
alto ciprés la mancha de su ramaje yerto.

La tarde está cayendo frente a los caserones
de la ancha plaza, en sueños. Relucen las vidrieras
con ecos mortecinos de sol. En los balcones
hay formas que parecen confusas calaveras.

La calma es infinita en la desierta plaza,
donde pasea el alma su traza de alma en pena.
El agua brota y brota en la marmórea taza.
En todo el aire en sombra no más que el agua suena.

Commentary

One of Machado's most assured poems where he creates a 'moodscape' and a meditation on passing time with associations of death: 'mancha', 'yerto', 'ciprés', mortecino', 'calaveras' in the symbolic closed space of the 'plaza'. The chipped fountain, the flowing water, the sunset all suggest the inexorable passage of time in a 'frame' where he can express the 'traza' of his 'alma en pena'. Again there is a painterly quality of this scene recalling the paintings of Zuloaga and Solana.

Published in *Renacimiento*, I, March 1907 under the title 'Pesadilla'. The poem has also been likened to the paintings of Giorgio de Chirico (1888–1978), founder of the Italian Scuola metafisica.

Alexandrine serventesios.

XCV

(COPLAS MUNDANAS)

Poeta ayer, hoy triste y pobre
filósofo trasnochado,
tengo en monedas de cobre
el oro de ayer cambiada.

Sin placer y sin fortuna,
pasó como una quimera
mi juventud, la primera ...
la sola, no hay más que una:
la de dentro es la de fuera.

Pasó como un torbellino,
bohemia y aborrascada,
harta de coplas y vino,
mi juventud bien amada.

Y hoy miro a las galerías
del recuerdo, para hacer
aleluyas de elegías
desconsoladas de ayer.

¡Adiós, lágrimas cantoras,
lágrimas que alegremente
brotabais, como en la fuente
las limpias aguas sonoras!

¡Buenas lágrimas vertidas
por un amor juvenil,
cual frescas lluvias caídas
sobre los campos de abril!

No canta ya el ruiseñor
de cierta noche serena;
sanamos del mal de amor
que sabe llorar sin pena.

Poeta ayer, hoy triste y pobre
filósofo trasnochado,
tengo en monedas de cobre
el oro de ayer cambiado.

Commentary

A further lament on time's erosion and lost opportunities where the gold (symbol of poetic inspiration: see the 'frutos de oro' motif across *SGOP*) has turned to base metal. He senses his early life was also empty. He may be referring to his bohemian phase in Seville and Paris in the 1890s. Once more he probes the 'galerías del recuerdo' (Symbolism) to frame an elegy and a farewell to his loss, cast in terms of flowing water, rain, springtime, the song of the nightingale. He also echoes, in the popular measure of the *copla*, the hidden pain of the *cantaor* who 'sabe llorar sin pena'. Thus his verses are a type of therapy.

Published in *Renacimiento*, I, March 1907 under the title 'De la vida (Coplas mundanas)'. Redondillas.

XCVI

(SOL DE INVIERNO)

Es mediodía. Un parque.
Invierno. Blancas sendas;
simétricos montículos
y ramas esqueléticas.

Bajo el invernadero,
naranjos en maceta,
y en su tonel, pintado
de verde, la palmera.

Un viejecillo dice,
para su capa vieja:
'¡El sol, esta hermosura de sol!' ...
Los niños juegan.

El agua de la fuente
resbala, corre y sueña
lamiendo, casi muda,
la verdinosa piedra.

Commentary

A reprise of poems LIII and LXXXI in a more staccato form of single words and short phrases. He combines many images of former poems – the park, garden, paths, bare branches, a glasshouse, plants in pots, an old man, children playing, a plashing fountain, mossy stone. In many ways these themes are redolent of Impressionist paintings which Machado would have seen in Paris or in the canvases of his friends and countrymen Santiago Rusiñol and Joaquín Sorolla. Possibly from memories of the Tuileries or the Madrid Retiro, these images become symbols of passing time, nostalgia, momentary longings and the timeless theme of children playing celebrated in poems III and VIII.

Published in *Renacimiento*, I, March 1907 and in *Tierra soriana*, 21-VII-1908. Romancillo in 7s in e-a.

Appendix

**A guide to a possible reading of Poem XCI,
'Húmedo está, bajo el laurel, el banco'**

The evocation of an autumnal garden or park is a commonplace in *Soledades. Galerías. Otros poemas* as in Symbolism in general. It is also a theme found in contemporary Impressionist painting. But is this poem Symbolist, merely a *paysage d'âme,* a *paisaje del alma*, a scene on which the poet overlays his feelings and emotions? In part, 'yes'. But there remain more profound issues embedded in a series of symbolic references that make the poem truly Symbolist. Consider the evocation of atmosphere and mood in the poem. It is one of decline and decay, a version of Machado's obsession with time and passing time: the year ('otoño'), the day ('tarde', 'ocaso') and the garden/park ('húmedo', 'verdinoso', 'empolvadas'). Thus there remains a sense of neglect, even abandonment, of age and the effects of passing time. Machado employs other devices to emphasise this process by slowing down the pace of the poem by a series of retentions. 1: The hendecasyllables are extended by running the verse over from one line to the next, *enjambement* (ll. 1–2, 5–6, 6–7, 9–10, 11–12). 2: Sentences are lengthened by the insertion of adverbial phrases of place which serve to slow the development of the sense: 'bajo el laurel' (v. 1); 'sobre el muro blanco' (v. 3); 'en su balcón' (v. 11); etc. 3: Further retentions: of the subordinate phrase in the third verse and the main clause in verse 13, for example, which supports the preceding description. 4: The retention of the subject in the opening stanza and its prolongation in the adverbial phrase in verse 2; the retained verb in verse 6, etc. These devices serve to slow the development of the poem and, thus, create a pensive atmosphere of nostalgia for what is lost and a tone of sombre meditation. The verbs, too, seem to lack a sense of progress, thus evoking a mood of reflection and sadness ending in a meditation and a looking backwards: 'voy recordando ...'. This mood is enhanced by the repetition of sibilants, the lulling 'l's and the 'ie's.

The poem begins on a real plane: the corner of an urban park with its stone furniture and its avenue of trees. But the scene is marked by time: the overgrown laurel, the bench green with moss, the white wall stained with rain, the ivy covered in what remains of the dust of summer, the long grass blown by the breeze, autumn, sunset, drying grapes. All these seem to suggest the loss of a former time of contentment and pleasure, perhaps love, all condemned by the preterite 'lavó' with its initial position and masculine rhyme. In this affirmation by negation we reach into the heart of Symbolist rhetoric. Note, for example, the typical use of adjectives in a pre-substantival position ('verdinosa piedra', 'empolvadas hojas', 'tibio aliento', 'estoica pipa'), which serve to enhance the emotional resonances and, thus, involve the noun itself. The norm in Spanish is for the adjective to follow the noun; Machado, like his friend Azorín, eschews the norm. Just as the dust of summer clings to the ivy, so the autumnal breezes retain their warmth. But the poet stands outside this 'conversation' of the breeze and the trees of the *alameda*. He cannot hear or share in this natural harmony. In poem LXVIII he relates that 'El viento huyó ...' and queries 'Alma, ¿qué has hecho de tu pobre huerto?' The *puntos suspensivos* in the final stanza here are, then, the equivalent of a sigh for what has been lost.

In the second part of the poem Machado presents the 'buen burgués', a *contrafigura* who, like the poet, strives to remain stoic as he surveys time's inexorable flow, an obsession in these verses (see LXXXI). We find similar stoical figures in the work of Jiménez and Azorín at this time. Yet, from the dank corner of the park the 'burgués', apart on his balcony, contemplates the golden sunset as it shafts down the avenue of trees and he smokes his 'estoica pipa', a transferred epithet, it is the man who is stoic. But why? Silence and solitude mark the verses of Machado and his *Helios* companions. Their *contrafiguras* take a kind of pleasure in their distress and the recognition of their loss of ideals. Stoicism is an act of will, of determination to see things through. Their creations are men of reflection rather than action. Thus the description of the park and the man is, at one level a physical reality, at another it creates an emotional scenario, a poem of self-contemplation and self-exploration. It creates the Symbolist *reino interior*. This *paysage d'âme* ends on a nostalgic seeking after the past, of youth, the poet's 'versos juveniles', a question prompted by the foregoing description of the park and the 'buen burgués'. Note the use of the continuous present in 'voy recordando ...' to emphasise the emotional impact, and the prolongation of the anxious search of memory. As in poems XIII and XXXV, his search and his dream are placed in passing time and here, too, evoked in a dreamlike halo of golden light, which suggests a sought-for tranquillity, possibly, as in many other poems of sunset, a goal that remains just out of reach. Note the contrast of initial gloom of the overgrown corner and the idealised sunset filled with light, a motif which runs through *SGOP*.

The final questions are directed to the poet himself, requiring a reply that is never forthcoming. Machado creates a tension between his quest for truth (reality) and acceptance (illusion and desire). He looks to a lost past ('fue', 'aquel'), distant in time, even space. His 'corazón sonoro' belongs to the past which he seeks in poem VI. Yet this surge of memory, provoked by the scene, is really a dream as he explains in poem LXXV. But 'sonoro' is a coupling of 'son' and 'oro', the voices he seeks to hear and the golden fruit and light he evokes in many poems. The second question is a more painful one, an emotional seeking for an answer rather than a factual reply: *quaestium* rather than *interrogatio*. The unifying element of the poem is now revealed in the reference to 'sombras gentiles'. But the final questions are fraught with tensions and anxiety, tensions reflected in the stresses. '¿Qué fue de aquel ...? offers three stresses at the outset of the line. In the following verse the pattern of stresses is even more uneven. Both these lines are quite unlike the other verses in the poem in terms of stress. This suggests an emotional point in the poem. But what are these 'sombras gentiles' in the context of the shift from 'alameda' to 'arboleda' and the evocation of a 'corazón sonoro'? On the real plane they are a play of light as the sun radiates down the wind-blown avenue of trees casting moving shadows, reminiscent of an Impressionist painting by Renoir. But is this related to the park? At one level 'yes'. But given frequent references across *SGOP* to fleeting figures, barely glimpsed, to golden fruit or golden drops (remember that Symbolism works not only in a single poem but across a whole collection through a series of repeated evocations), these shades are symbolic. The real plane becomes the evoked plane. With the conjunction of fleeting shadows, sound, gold and woods (rather than *alameda*, Machado suggests (a key to Symbolist practice) the poetic Muses who dwell in the Woods of Helicon on the flanks of Mount Parnassus, home to the God of Poetry and Inspiration, Apollo. In these woods the trees hang with golden fruit or drops of gold which are the instruments they bring to poets in the form of inspiration. And this takes us back to the laurel and the empty moss-grown bench beneath it at the outset of the poem. The laurel was sacred to Apollo but the god no longer sits on his throne. His seat is moss-grown, neglected, his laurel crown now covered in dust and smears of rain, his power absent. And with the fleeing Muses any hope of recovering the inspirational power of his 'versos juveniles'. The poet's heart (imagination, poetic soul) was filled with 'son' and 'oro', the golden drops of inspiration. Now it is not and the poet seeks to rediscover that poetic power. The poem, then, is a lament, of loss, of waning inspiration, of the ability to frame his insights. Yet, in the final analysis, he has written an exceptional poem. Like Alfred de Musset in his *Un merle blanc* where he laments over an extensive poem his failure to be able to write one, Machado, too, has achieved just that. In the final analysis we have a highly suggestive and complex poem in the language of genuine Symbolism. The desire to recover what Machado senses he has lost begins in poem I and appears across the whole collection. Here he exploits language and syntax to offer the reader an insight into the dilemma faced by a poet who senses that his powers are insufficient to take on the task of renovating a discredited poetic practice of the previous generation and, in so doing, he believed, he might regenerate his fellow men as he shared his own doubts with a nation that doubted itself.

For an extensive examination of this poem see Cardwell 1987.

Temas de debate y discusión

Discusión

1. Considera el uso machadiano de las imágenes de lienzos, espaciosos cerrados, parques, jardines, arboledas, etc. ¿Qué efecto poético busca el poeta?
2. ¿Qué significa Machado cuando habla de sus 'galerías del alma'? Considera las imágenes correlativas que emplea: espejos, prismas, cavernas, senderos, horizontes, espacios cerrados, etc.
3. Identifica las imágenes que usa Machado para evocar sus emociones y sentimientos más íntimos.
4. Escribe una lista de los elementos (naturaleza, realidades cotidianos, memorias, clasicismos, etc.) que se combinan para crear un poema simbolista o una serie de poemas que combinan los mismos elementos. Considera también cómo estos elementos contribuyen a articular la visión poética: a) del propio poeta y b) del artista luchando en una guerra literaria.
5. Escribe un comentario sobre el poema número XCIV empleando el ejemplo crítico ofrecido en el Apéndice de esta edición.
6. *SGOP* ofrece una mezcla de imágenes decadentistas, clásicas y místicas. Considera cómo Machado las emplea para evocar su viaje emocional hacia una unión con un Otro personal o un dios personal.
7. Considera la imagen del payaso o titiritero en *SGOP*. ¿Por qué las emplea? ¿Qué efecto crea el empleo de estas imágenes?

Debate

1. ¿De qué manera expresa Machado su sentido de la impotencia artística?
2. ¿De qué manera se relaciona SGOP con las preocupaciones artísticas del momento literario de 1902–1907?
3. ¿Por qué se escriben la mayoría de los poemas en versos de prosodia tradicional?
4. ¿De qué manera es lícito leer SGOP como la expresión de la educación del poeta en la familia Machado, la Institución Libre, el ambiente intelectual del fin de siglo, y sus relaciones con Unamuno, Jiménez y Azorín?
5. ¿Son los poemas de SGOP, como sugiere el título, la expresión de una soledad emocional de un poeta solitario o forman parte, como sugiere el poeta, de la guerra literaria de los jóvenes artistas del nuevo siglo?
6. ¿Es posible hablar de Machado como un poeta místico?

Selected vocabulary

abatir, to demolish, fell, knock down
abeja, bee
abejorro, bumblebee
aborrecido, hated, loathed, boring
abrevar, to water, give to drink
acechar, to spy on, watch
acequia, irrigation ditch
acero, steel
acibarado, made bitter
acompasado, rhythmic, regular
adamantino, adamantine, very hard
adusto, scorching, severe, austere
afilado, sharpened
agrio, sharp (of sound)
aguardar, to await
águila, eagle
aguja, needle
alado, winged
álamo, poplar tree
alarido, shriek, cry
alba, dawn
albahaca, basil (a herb)
albor, dawn
alborear, to dawn
alborotar, to disturb, stir up
alcanzar, to reach, attain
alcoba, bedroom
alcor, hill
aleluyas, popular song sheets
alfanje, cutlass, sword
algarabía, gabble, gibberish
algazara, din, clamour, uproar
aliento, breath
aljaba, quiver for arrows
almendro, almond tree
alumbrar, to light up
amapola, poppy
amargo, bitter
amargura, bitterness
amarillear, to go yellow
amarrado, moored (of boat)
amenguar, to diminish, lessen
ancho, wide
angosto, narrow
añorar, to long for
antesala, antechamber, lobby
antorcha, torch
apagarse, to put out (a light, flame or fire)
apartarse de, to withdraw from
apestar, to infect, corrupt
apolillado, moth-eaten
apuesto, neat, elegant
arboleda, grove of trees
arena, sand
arnés, armour, harness
aromado, fragrant, scented
aromar, to effuse fragrance

arrancar, to pull up, root or draw out
arrebatado, hasty, sudden, violent
arrebol, red glow, flush
arrinconado, remote, forgotten
arroyo, stream, brook
arrugado, wrinkled
arrumbado, neglected, set aside
ascuas, embers, ashes
asomar, to peer over, appear, stand out
asordado, deafened
áspero, sour, tart, bitter (of smell)
atar, to tie
ataúd, coffin
atracado, moored (of a boat)
atril, lectern, bookstand
atrio, inner courtyard, atrium
aturdir, to stun, daze, bewilder
aura, dawn
aúreo, golden
avena, oats
aventar, to fan; to winnow
averiguar, to ascertain, discover
azada, hoe
azar, chance, fate
azogue, mercury, quicksilver
azorado, alarmed
barbitaheño, with a reddish beard
barrer, to sweep clean
bermejo, bright red
blandir, to brandish, flourish
blanquecino, whitish
borbollante, bubbling
bordón, string instrument
borrado, erased, rubbed out, indistinct
borroso, blurred, indistinct
bostezo, yawn
bóveda, vault, dome
brasa, hot coal
brotar, to well up
bruñir, to burnish, polish
bucle, curl, ringlet
bullir, to boil
cabalgar, to ride (a horse)
cabellera, long hair
caja, box, coffin
calabaza, pumpkin, gourd
calado, soaked to the skin
calavera, skull
calcinar, reduce to ashes
calentar, to warm
cálido, hot
calleja, narrow street
calvo, bald
campanario, bell tower
campanita, small bell
caña, cane
cancela, wrought-iron gate
cándida, simple, ingenuous, innocent
candil, lamp
cangilón, bucket on a water wheel
cantar, to sing
cántaro, pitcher
capullo, cocoon, bud (of flower)
carcoma, death watch beetle, wood worm
carcomido, worm-eaten
cárdeno, purple, violet
carmín, crimson red
carnicero, carnivorous
carretera, road
cartel, poster
casco, helmet, head
caserón, large house
cauce, riverbed

cazador, huntsman
cegar, to blind
ceniciento, ashen
ceñido, tight fitting
cenit, zenith
ceniza, ashes
ceño, frown, scowl
centella, spark
centenario, centennial, centenarian
cera, wax
césped, lawn
chillar, to screech, squawk
chispeante, sparkling, emitting sparks
chispear, to sparkle, crackle (of fire)
chisporroteo, throwing out sparks
chopo, black poplar tree
ciervo, stag
cigarra, cicada
cigüeña, stork
cipresal, cypress grove
cizaña, tares (wild weeds)
clarear, to brighten, light up
clepsidra, water clock
colegiales, schoolchildren
colgar, to hang up
colmena, bee hive
colmenar, apiary
concha, shell, conch
conseja, story, tale
consuelo, consolation
copa, crown of a tree
copla, ballad, popular song
corcel, steed
cordel, cord
corolla, corolla
coronar, to crown
corza, doe
crepúsculo, sunset
crespón, crêpe
cripta, crypt
crisol, crucible
cristal, water (poetic); window pane; crystal
cuadro, picture; frame
cuerda, cord
cuita, care
cumbre, pinnacle, summit
cursilería, bad taste, vulgarity
daguerrotipo, daguerreotype, sepia photograph
dalia, dahlia
deletreo, interpretation of text, spelling
derruido, demolished, ruined
desamarrado, unmoored, untied (of boats)
descansar, to rest
desconfiar, to mistrust
desdén, disdain
desdeñoso, scornful, disdainful
desengaño, disillusion; disappointment
desgarrado, torn, ripped, tattered
desgarrar, to tear, rip, crush
deshojar, to defoliate, strip of leaves
destartalado, untidy, dilapidated
devanar, to wind, spin
diamantino, diamond-like, glittering
disparatado, absurd, nonsensical
divagar, to digress, wander, ramble
doncellita, maiden, young girl

dormitar, to doze
duelo, grief, sorrow
élitro, grasshopper, cicada
emborracharse, to get drunk
emboscada, ambush
embozado, covered up to the eyes
embriagar, to inebriate
empañar, to steam up (of windows, glass, etc.), to mist
empolvado, dusty
enano, dwarflike
encaje, lace
encina, holm oak
enhiesto, erect, upright
enjaulado, caged
enmarañar, to tangle
enroscar, to coil around, twist
enturbiarse, to make muddy or cloudy
ermita, hermitage
escombros, rubble, debris
escueto, plain, unadorned, bare
espantar, to frighten, scare
esparcir, to scatter, spread
espina, thorn
espuela, spur
espuma, foam, spume
esquivo, shy, reserved, aloof
estepa, steppe, plateau
estéril, sterile
estival, summerlike
estupor, stupor; astonishment
exprimir, to squeeze out
falucho, fishing boat
famélico, starving
fanal, lantern, beacon
fanfarrón, boastful, blustering
férreo, ferrous, ironlike
fiera, wild beast

fingir, to pretend
florido, flowering
fontana, fountain
forjar, to forge
fosa, grave, trench
fulgir, to dazzle, glow
fulgurar, to glow, gleam
gacela, gazelle; Arab song
garabato, hook, scribble (in writing)
gaviota, seagull
gayo, merry, gay
geranio, geranium
girar, to turn
glorieta, bower, arbour
golondrina, swallow (a bird)
goloso, sweet-toothed
golpear, to strike, hit
gota, drop (of liquid)
grueso, fat, large
guerrero, warrior
gusano, worm
hada, fairy, spirit
hálito, breath, sigh
harapiento, ragged, tattered
harén, harem
hastío, weariness; loathing
helado, frozen
hender, cleave, slip through a wave (of boats)
hervir, to boil
hiedra, ivy
hierbabuena, mint (herb)
hilar, to spin
hilera (en), in a file
hilo, thread
hinchado, swollen
histrión, actor, player, buffoon
hogar, hearth, home

hondo, deep
huella, print, trace
huerto, orchard
hueso, bone
humareda, cloud of smoke
humear, to emit smoke, fume
hundir, sink, plunge
huso, spindle, bobbin (in weaving)
imprimirse, to imprint, stamp
infierno, hell
ingrave, weightless
inopia, poverty
inquietud, disquiet, unease
irrisorio, derisory, ridiculous
jota, Aragonese dance
juguete, toy, plaything
junco, bullrush, reed
junqueral, reed bed
lactescente, milky
ladrón, thief
lagar, wine press
lágrima, tear
laguna, lake, lagoon
lánguido, languid, limp
lanza, lance
lares, ancestral hearth, home
lecho, bed
levita, frock coat
leyenda, legend, tale
libraco, boring or worthless book
librote, tome, heavy book
lienzo, canvas, picture
ligero, light, thin
limo, mud, slime
limonero, lemon tree
limpio, clean
linfa, water (poetic)
lirio, iris (flower)
llama, flame

llanura, plain, flat lands
loba, she-wolf
lograr, to achieve
loma, hillock, low ridge
lomo, back of a mule
lucero, star
lumbre (noun), light, glow
luminaria, lamp; inspired person
luminoso, luminous
lunático, mad, lunatic, moonstruck
macabro, macabre
maceta, flower pot
macizo, massive, solid
madera, cut wood, timber
mago (noun), magician; (adj), magical
maldecir, to curse
malhaya, damn!
maltratado, ill-treated
manantial, spring, source (of water)
mancha, stain, blemish
manchado, stained
mansamente, gently, softly
manzanar, apple orchard
marchito, withered
marino, marine, of the sea
mármol, marble
marmóreo, marble-like, marmoreal
martillo, hammer
matutino (adj), of the morning
mazurca, mazurka (Hungarian dance)
mechón, lock of hair
medroso, fearful, timid
mendigo, beggar
mentiroso, deceitful

mesón, country inn
mezquino, mean, poor spirited
mirador, vantage point
mirto, myrtle bush
mohoso, rusty, mouldy
monorritmo, single rhythm
montículo, small hill
morada (noun), dwelling
morado (adj), purple, violet
mordido, gnawed
moreno, dark-haired
mortecino, failing, dying
moruno, Moorish
mudo, dumb
muelle (adj), soft, springy
musgo, moss
mustio, faded, withered
naranjito, small orange tree
nardo, spikenard (flower)
nave, ship
negrear, to turn black
negruzco, blackish
nevasca, snowstorm, blizzard
noria, well (water with waterwheel drawn by a mule)
ocaso, sunset
odio, hatred
olmo, elm tree
oloroso, scented, fragrant
órbita, eye-socket
oriente, Orient; morning star
orilla, river bank, shore
oscurecer, to darken, grow dim
óvalo, oval shaped
palmos de tierra, a measure of land
palpitar, to throb, beat
al paño, an actor waiting in the wings

pardo, grey-brown
paredón, thick wall
párpado, eyelid
pavor, fear
pavura, fear
pedantón al paño, an opinionated ridiculous person
peluquero, barber, hairdresser
pensiles, flowers
peregrino, pilgrim
persiana, slatted shutter (of windows)
pertinaz, persistent, obstinate
petenera, Spanish dance and song
pífano, fife (musical pipe)
pintarrajeado, daubed
piqueta, pickaxe
pisado, trodden down
pitagórico, Pythagorian
placidez, placidity
plácido, placid, calm
plañido, grieving
plañir, grieve, mourn
plateado, silvery
plazoleta, small plaza
plegaria, prayer
podrido, rotten, putrid
polvoriento, dusty
poma, apple
pompa de jabón, soap bubble
postigo, wicket gate, postern
presa, prey
pretil, parapet; edge of a fountain
prisa, hustle, hurry
quebrado, broken
quebrar, to break, smash
quedarse, to remain
queja, complaint
quimera, chimera, phantom

racimo, bunch, cluster (of fruit/flowers)
rama, branch
raudo, impetuous, rushing in
rebato, call to arms, alarm call
rebosar, to overflow
rebotar, to upset, bounce
rebullir, to stir
rechinar, to grate, creak
recio, harsh, loud
redondo, round
reja, iron window bars
remanso, pool, backwater
reparar, to observe, notice
repercutir, to bounce off, echo
repicar, to ring out, peal
reposar, to rest
reprimir, to check, repress
requemado, scorched, parched
resbalar, to slip, slither, bounce
resol, glare of the sun
retablo, stage set
reverdecer, grow green anew
revuelta, bend, turn in the road
rezar (verb), to pray; (noun), a prayer
rezo, prayer
ribera, riverbank
rincón, corner
risueño, smiling
rizado, curly
rodar, to tumble along/down
roído, eaten away, gnawed
romero, pilgrim
rosal, rose bush
rostro, face
rubio, blonde, golden
ruiseñor, nightingale
rutilante, shining, sparkling
saeta, arrow
sagital, of arrows
salado, salty, witty, amusing
salmo, psalm
salmodiar, to sing psalms
salterio, psalter
sanar, to heal, cure
sandalia, sandal
sangrar, to bleed
sangriento, bloody
sanguinario, bloodthirsty, cruel
sauce, willow tree
sazonado, ripe, mellow, tasty
sediento, thirsty
semblante, face, appearance
sembrador, sower
sementero, of seedtime, time for sowing
sempiterno, everlasting
senda, path
sendero, path
sepulturero, grave digger
serpear, to wind
sien, temple, forehead
sierpe, serpent, snake
sitio, place, site
sobrado, superfluous, excessive
sombrear, to shade
sombrío, gloomy, shady
soñar, to dream
soñoliento, dreamy
soplar, to blow, puff
soplo, gust, puff
sopor, drowsiness, lethargy
soriano, from Soria
surcar, to plough, groove
tahur, gambler
tálamo, marriage bed
talante, mood, disposition

183

talar, to prune
talares, pruned, shaped (trees, plants)
tañer, to ring (of bells)
tañido, sound of bells
tapia, mud wall (of yards and gardens)
temer, to fear
terrón, clod of earth, sod
terso, smooth, polished
testuz, head (of a bull)
tierno, tender, soft
tijera (adj), noise of scissors
timbre, bell
tiritar, to shiver
titerero, puppet
tizón, burning piece of wood
tocado, toilet set, headdress
tonel, barrel, cask
torbellino, storm
tormenta, storm
torreón, large tower
tortuoso, winding, torturous
torvo, grim, stern
tosco, coarse, rough
trasnochado, wan, haggard
tremir, to tremble
trigo, corn, wheat
tristón, gloomy, deeply sad
trocar, to change, switch
trofeo, trophy
tronar, to thunder, rumble
trono, throne; noise of thunder
trova, song of minstrel
turbio, turbid, cloudy (of liquids)
tutelar, as a guardian
umbral, threshold
umbroso, shady
ungido, anointed
usurpar, to usurp, encroach on
vagar, to wander
vela, sail (of ship), candle
velita, small candle
vellón, copper alloy; type of thick wool
vellorita, part of a flower
velludo, hairy, shaggy, wool like
vender, to sell
ventanal, large window
ventisca, snowstorm
verdiflorido, flowering green
vereda, path, lane
verter, to pour our
veste, dress
vid, grapevine
voltear, roll over
voraz, voracious
yema, fingertip; leaf bud
yerto, stiff, rigid
yunque, anvil
zarzuela, light opera
zumo, juice